CULMINATION OF A MIRACLE:

A Book Series Compilation

By

Daniel K. Arnold

Culmination of A Miracle:

Preface

I am Daniel K. Arnold and I am a living testimony to the quote, "He who began a good work in you will be faithful to complete it."

Jesus has been working in my life since before I was born. The devil has tried to thwart this, but God is in control!

You may say, "Than isn't He controlling us if God is in control?"

By all means no. God wrote the story; we live it out. I intend to play the part God has selected me for because it's awesome. That's not control; that's an honor!

In the Book of Jeremiah of the Bible, God says, "Before I formed thee in the belly I knew thee; and before thou camest forth out of the womb I sanctified thee, *and* I ordained thee a prophet unto the nations (Jeremiah 1:5)."

God is no respecter of persons; He does not discriminate. He has a plan for everyone and everything.

"For God so loved the world that He gave His One and Only Son that whosoever believeth in Him shall not perish, but have eternal life (John 3:16)."

God loves you as He loves me. The pages of this epic book series reveals that love through the complex Super Hero character of Mister Energy Plus, who becomes Black Bird Ops (both characters suffering with mental illness), but ultimately converts into a healthly, sound mind unique hero that God knew from the beginning as Daniel.

Daniel means in Hebrew, "God will be my Judge."

God is surely in control. He is the only one to love me perfectly and the only one with the right to decide my eternal destination.

Learn from this hero how one might live extravagantly and not fall into the pitfalls he learned from falling into and getting out of by the grace of God, remembering that "A righteous man falls down seven times and gets back up again (Proverbs)."

God loves you and has a high calling on your life. Do not give up. You are not an accident no matter what the world says!

If God can take a prideful, self-centered fool like my old person and make him into a hero, He can do the same for you if you are willing.

The story continues now; it is being written right now! So play the part to the glory of God. Have faith and <u>do not give up</u>!

Culmination of A Miracle:

A Brief Walk-Through

To better understand this world, we begin with the first book, The Super Hero Manual.

Introduced in this tale is heroics from the perspective of sickness. The character (me) learns to cope as best he can with his life riding the fence between epic and less than epic disability—remembering that God is in control. The book is broken up into chapters that dive into the mesh of mental illness and spirituality culture. A very intriguing world that is part of the puzzle.

On to EverChanging, Book II in the epic Super Hero Manual Series, Culmination of A Miracle.

As a Super Hero I lay out the challenges of holding onto my faith while my health deteriorates as best I can—learning not to give up on the plan God has for my life. Laid out are case study examples of the disorders, Type I Bipolar Disorder (as played by Mister Energy Plus) and Schizoaffective (as played by Black Bird Ops). In this fascinating tale, God continues to be glorified from the perspective of the Super Hero at that time in his journey.

Through much editing, toil and conviction we come to Obey God, a prequel to the Super Hero

Manual Series, modified that becomes ever-more an integral teaching of his beliefs, based on truths from the Bible. This book is a must read, must have, must do, that will change your life again and again! Do not miss the opportunity to read it cover to cover.

Ending in the Present Tense, Confessions of A Healed Man Book, we enter into the inner, top secret sanctum of my adventures, thoughts, life aspirations—only available in the complete set! The context of all previous books in The Super Hero Manual Series, this book will finally reveal the secret to Spirit-powered life liberation into becoming a healthy hero for the glory of God.

Take this ride with an open-mind, in proper order from first book to last book, beginning to end, for it was inspired by God and is still being lived out by Yours Truly.
I now present: Culmination of A Miracle: A Book Series Compilation. "We walk by faith not by sight." Be blessed!

Love in Christ

Daniel K. Arnold

THE SUPER HERO MANUAL

By

Daniel K. Arnold

The Super Hero Manual: Table of Contents

THE SUPER HERO MANUAL

by

Daniel K. Arnold

The Super Hero Manual

Chapter 1: Introduction

What is the definition of the words, "Super," "Hero" and "Disability?"

<u>Super</u> is defined by Collins English Dictionary as being, "informal, outstanding; exceptionally fine."

<u>Hero</u> is defined as being, "a man distinguished by exceptional courage, nobility, fortitude, etc."

<u>Disability</u> is defined as being, "lack of adequate power, strength, or physical or mental <u>ability</u>; incapacity."

"Through the Eyes of the Super Hero" is as it says. It describes an outstanding group of people who share the reality of a disability—people who are able to do exceptional feats with exceptional courage despite hindrances. These people have a legacy to leave in shaping the world. They matter and the impact that they makes is nothing short of legendary. Maybe the work is behind the scenes, like the Invisible Man or perhaps they are only known among those they rescue. Perhaps only God can see the efforts made by the individuals who at times are almost completely marginalized by society. This steadfast spirit is still nothing short of the makings of a Super Hero.

Thus the Super Hero is born—tales within the pages of articles that may shed light on the potential in us all if you simply read between the lines.

The Super Hero Manual

Chapter 2: New 'Recruits'

Orientation:

"Why am I here? What did I do? Why am I a patient?"

"Come with us Jed. You are showing delusions of grandeur. You need to come to the white room to intake. To better serve you, we are going to have to ask you some questions about yourself."

"But I just want a pastor first. You don't understand the importance of clergy. All you want is to give me drugs to pay your superiors."

Body:

A patient entering a mental health hospital for the first time may find it to be a place that has every resource he/she does not want.

He/she may be aligned to the health science of nutrition and be desperate for supplements or organic food. The patient may be aligned to the health science of psychology and just want a friend to talk to who understands by his/her bedside. He/she may be aligned to the health science of pharmacology and want to pop ten 'ativans' in an attempt to calm down. Or like me, when I did my first intake at a mental hospital, the patient may believe in standing on spirituality alone—believing spiritual guidance will solve all problems immediately.

In the Bible, there was a man named Jesus who duplicated organic fish (Nutrition), who reasoned with the masses through analogies (Psychology), who told his disciples to "take a little wine" along on their journey (Pharmacology), who delivered a demon-possessed man with authority from God (Spiritual Guidance).

All four of these health sciences were applied in a reasonable orderly manner. There was and is a place for them all.

If you are entering this minimum to high security facility hospital or crisis unit, know that although your welcome squad is stressed out, they typically do care about your well-being. Be patient with them. Their treatment of your heroic condition will be more helpful than you first imagined.

(Nutrition) You will be provided quite a selection of healthy food.

(Psychology) On a limited basis, your friends and family will be able to come visit you. (So make a list of their names and phone numbers while you have a cell phone, including your pastor.)

(Pharmacology) Your prior medication and new medication will be tightly regulated for your best possible health outcome.

(Spiritual Guidance) A chaplain will most likely be able to visit you, so make an appointment now. Lastly, if you don't have a Bible, ask for one. There should be a full Bible on the premises.

Enjoy your stay! It's a great opportunity to make friends for life and to get to know Jesus through, resources, friends, family, suffering, clergy, the Bible, and this book.

Take your badly needed rest. From here on you will learn the art of being a Super Hero.

The Super Hero Manual

Chapter 3: The Art of Being a Super Hero

Forget everything you learned about being great. You may lose all your friends, but the ones you keep you will call family. Do not, I repeat, Do not call yourself better than 'ordinary' people. It does not matter if you have saved ten people from a burning building, the glory belongs to God.

If you do not know God, then this is a great time for you to be given an opportunity. "Seek the LORD while you can find him. Call on him now while he is near.." (Isaiah 55:6)

Jesus has come to rescue you in your desperation—to meet you where you are at. He died on the cross for your sins. He paid a real price so that you can be spiritually free.

Have you been down that road before? Does it seem Jesus has let you down?

Life is full of difficulties—even Job and King David in the Bible faced threat of death, but God saw them through.

On my first intake, I needed to ask myself the question as to whether I really knew God—or whether I was acting as a Sly Villain.

Despite hardships, persecutions, and difficulties, do you really know Jesus as more than a character in a book, but as a personal Comforter? He says, "Come to me all ye who are weary and heavy-laden and I will give you rest." (Matthew 11:28) Let Jesus minister in your life today by giving your whole heart to Him.

"If you confess with your mouth that Jesus is Lord and believe in your heart that God raised him from the dead, you will be saved." (Romans 10:9)

It's that simple. It's that hard. It's living to make Jesus the Super Star and letting Him lift you up in due time. Take a back seat, smile, and anticipate the places you'll go, the people you'll reach for God's glory. If you are not yet converted to the role of hero, whether or not you have "super powers," keep on reading. Sit back. Get caught up in the story and know you are loved.

The Super Hero Manual

Chapter 4: All Things are Possible!

Abstract:

What are the signs to look for in a person who is going to help change the world? Everyone has someone they admire and look to for aid in setting a measurement for what they aspire to be. Are the symptoms of spiritual greatness potential (SGP) large shoe size, being first-born, being born into privilege, or natural charisma?

Looking at the case studies of 7 "Super Heroes" of the faith and various Scriptures, this study hypothesized that SGP = W + R (POHL), but came to the conclusion that SGP cannot be determined by man.

SGP=Spiritual Greatness Potential

W= Weakness

R= Reliance

POHL= Power of His Love.

Introduction:

"I'll say it again—it is easier for a camel to go through the eye of a needle than for a rich person to enter the Kingdom of God!" The disciples were astounded. "Then who in the world can be saved?"

they asked. Jesus looked at them intently and said, "Humanly speaking, it is impossible. But with God everything is possible (Matthew 9:24-26)."

Peering at this passage, it is evident that in the Kingdom of God, it is hard "for a rich man to enter the Kingdom of God." However, POHL trumps all rules in the spiritual as well as carnal world. The Power of Jesus's Love, as Jesus is God makes all things possible.

"Remember, dear brothers and sisters, that few of you were wise in the world's eyes or powerful or wealthy when God called you. Instead, God chose things the world considers foolish in order to shame those who think they are wise. And he chose things that are powerless to shame those who are powerful. God chose things despised by the world, things counted as nothing at all, and used them to bring to nothing what the world considers important. As a result, no one can ever boast in the presence of God (1 Corinthians 1:26-29)."

Foolishness, or weakness, is a factor to in determining whether someone will be used by God to accomplish great things. The greater "W' is, the more God can use the circumstance to show that change is coming about not by that vessel's (person's) power, but by God's power. Working with Kingdom Principles the opposite of the

Natural's Principles, those who are weak are just about better equipped to demonstrate God's greatness than those who are naturally strong. However, we cannot forget Matthew 9:26 that says, "… But with God everything is possible."

Looking back at the equation, SGP= W + R(POHL), we see that although Weakness plays a positive role in Spiritual Growth Potential, Reliance on the Power of His Love has an infinitely greater impact.

"My conscience is clear, but that doesn't prove I'm right. It is the Lord himself who will examine me and decide. So don't make judgments about anyone ahead of time—before the Lord returns. For he will bring our darkest secrets to light and will reveal our private motives. Then God will give to each one whatever praise is due. (1 Corinthians 4:4-5)"

It is God that makes the ultimate difference in SGP. And to even create an equation to determine the difference someone will make in their life is man's foolishness because it limits God's power to make a difference in that person's life.

Case Studies of Seven Underestimated Bible Heroes:

Pen Name	Weakness	The Facts
"Homeless" Christ Crucified		
	Born In a Manger	Savior of the World
	Homeless	Died on the Cross for our Sins
	Accused of Demon Possession	
		God In Flesh
The Dreamer		
	Symptoms of Grandiosity	Dreams came to pass!
	Sold into Slavery	Relentless despite persecution.
	Sent to Prison	Becomes a merciful ruler.

Shepherd Boy

Runt of the Family	Chosen King of The Chosen Nation
Job Experience is with Sheep	A Man After God's Own Heart

The Loud Mouth Fisherman

Impulsivity and Pride	Known for Denying Christ 3 Times
Job Experience is with Fish	Walking on Water
	Died a Martyr's Death for Jesus

Locusts and Honey

Violated Social Norms in Dress and Behavior	Prepared the Way for the Coming of the Lord
	Great in the Kingdom yet the Least

Widow 2 Cents

Impoverished Widow	"Put in more than all the rest."

Blind Paul

Persecutor of Christians	Suffered Greatly for the Sake of the Gospel
Went Blind	Wrote Approximately Half the New Testament

Source: The Holy Bible, NLT, 2007.

Conclusion:

No equation can be used to determine someone's potential in the Kingdom of God. That would equate to judging. But the LORD said to Samuel, "Don't judge by his appearance or height, for I have rejected him. The LORD doesn't see things the way you see them. People judge by outward appearance, but the LORD looks at the heart (1 Samuel 16:7)."

It is not about the card that we are dealt in this life that determines who we become or other's perceptions of us. "All things are possible with God" and without Him nothing can be accomplished.

The Super Hero Manual

Chapter 5: Accommodation and Compliance

Abstract:

Every individual is unique. There is no normal. As with Super Heroes, individuals come one-of-a-kind requiring accommodations from both a civilized society and from a loving, Biblical society. As seen in last study, weakness according the world's standards must not be pre-judged as a sign of less potential.

The tricky line is balancing the accommodation society knows a person needs with varying levels of spiritual faith among the masses. A danger arises with pressure to convert to no medication and all faith or all medication and no faith. When a Super Hero's condition falls to the level where medical compliance is court-mandated, great steps of faith are no longer associated with just the potential of a good testimony, but more the potential of both death and breaking the law.

The purpose of this article is to point out the place of contradiction an all or nothing faith-believer can be placed in. In addition, I want to stress the importance of faith in God to heal at times and at most times the faith to let the medicine that God has inspired work, uninterrupted.

Case Study:

I will take a moment to reflect upon my life. My name is Daniel and I have been non-compliant with my doctors' medication prescription about ten times. Each time I went off the medication, I anticipated the best. I was 'healed' and I wasn't ashamed to tell everyone about it. Every time I was medication non-compliant, if I did not return to medication soon, I ended up hospitalized. In addition, I noticed a falling away in relationship with friendships with individuals and with churches. This situation alienated me from many people.

Body:

Super Heroes are created in such a way where they have great talents, great abilities that are unique. As in the study on "Widow 2 Cents" in the last chapter, extreme deficits are interpreted differently in the Kingdom of God than in the Kingdom of this world. What can be seen as lack in "Widow 2 Cents" was seen by Jesus as putting "in more than all the rest" (in the offering).

With this Kingdom mentality, society has no place to judge a Super Hero on what contribution they can make to society nor what accommodations they need.

Fictional Example:

Jenny is riding down the street in her wheelchair and someone steals it from her because they want to build faith in her for healing.

Does this not sound absurd? Jenny was functioning well with her accommodation, but someone in society made a judgment call on her based on his/her perception of her faith. The individual believed he/she was helping Jenny, when in fact he/she was only further handicapping her and mortifying her.

Does this mean that there should be no exercises of faith? By all means no! However, more Scripture should be looked at then Christ's miracles that healed all the sick He came in contact with. After all, He is God and we are not. We cannot blame the victim who does not get healed for lack of faith. God's "strength is made perfect in weakness as the Apostle Paul said. Paul had to deal with a messenger of satan and this was his response. Despite this mental, spiritual, whatever it was ailment, Paul did great things in the Kingdom of God—albeit from human perception.

Conclusion:

What someone accomplishes and his/her level of faith is determined by God and God alone. The situation of a Super Hero with a mental or physiological kryptonite taking medicine is similar to anyone fasting what will destroy him/her. It is giving the brain the chemicals it lacks.

With modern technology, we cannot deny one man his lithium, that naturally occurs in the brain and give another man a prosthetic leg. We must give Super Heroes the accommodations that fit their needs so they can accomplish the Heroics that they were born to do.

The Super Hero Manual

Chapter 6: Finding Balance and Purpose

Abstract:

This study demonstrates the need to for a Super Hero to find balance in a sound mind, work, and looking to the Holy Bible for stability.

Introduction:

Some cannot get out of bed without their morning cup of coffee. "Moderation in everything" is how the saying goes. Caffeine wakes up many and some are put out by a little tryptophan at night. These chemicals are naturally occurring in various foods and drinks. The Super Hero has a bit more of some chemicals and a deficiency of others at various levels in the brain.

Is this abnormal or something extra special? As my mother once said, "God made you and God made no junk." There are no wasted humans as long as humankind lives with a purpose.

Chapter 6 looks at three sections of the Bible with balance and purpose in mind.

Body:

Section I: (2 Timothy 1:7)

"For God has not given us a spirit of fear and timidity, but of power, love, and self-discipline."

First, we need not be afraid of what others think. For if God is in us, we as Super Heroes have not just been given a sound mind, but of power and love and well. As David in Psalms said, "With my God I can scale a wall."

Super Heroes have been given distinct gifts that vary from intense empathy to one-of-a-kind boldness and enthusiasm. This makes the Super Hero just plain awesome!

"I am fearfully and wonderfully made." (Psalm 139:14)

Yes, the Super Heroes have weaknesses, but in their weakness, God's power can be seen with epic proportions.

Section II: (2 Thessalonians 3:10-11)

"Even while we were with you, we gave you this command: "Those unwilling to work will not get to eat" Yet we hear that some of you are living idle lives, refusing to work and meddling in other people's business."

Work is important for a person to find purpose in his/her life, balance, and to fulfill God's command. Collins English Dictionary 2009, first defines "work" as "physical or mental effort directed towards doing or making something" and secondarily as, "paid employment at a job or a trade, occupation, or profession."

With a shortage of careers in some regions, it is at times near impossible to fulfill definition two, but definition one is always possible. Definition one work can be defined as anything from trade school, to diligently putting your hands to a hobby to invest in others, to volunteering, to working for money. The Super Hero may be resting from a great adventure, but on some level they can still put forth work—even if it is making a conscious effort to better understand him or herself. Idleness is to be avoided, but "working" to make positive steps towards the future is once again, awesome.

Section III: (Ecclesiastes 3:1-8)

"For everything there is a season, a time for every activity under heaven."
If it's Christmas Time, people want to hear Christmas Music, but not during Valentines Day. The same goes true for the behavior of a Super Hero. Chicken Little need not cry out that the sky is falling when it's not. If a Super Hero is having a

medical emergency, he/she should seek help even though he/she is a Super Hero. Everyone has down days and everyone has up days.

Creating a balanced schedule that becomes complicated could be taxing for the perfectionist, but just right for the disorderly Super Hero. Once again, everything must be done in the proper season.

Conclusion:

Super Heroes need to take care of themselves like anyone else. They sometimes need special accommodations and days to take a rest. Super Heroes are human like everyone else.

The Super Hero Manual

Chapter 7: The Etiquette of Confidentiality

Abstract:

When knowledge of personal medical diagnoses and medication intake are used as weapons of discrimination, the information becomes confidential—no one else's business but the consumer and primary care doctor.

Body:

Some information belongs off-limits when it has the potential of being used by others to harm the consumer. Unfortunately, career applications are going the way of beginning to ask for this type of information—with fears that potential employees could be a liability on the job. Nevertheless, for the most part this information can be kept secret.

Imagine that every time Tony has a bad day at work, instead of asking him why he feels miserable, people pry and ask him if he is taking his medication. At this place in time, Tony is being reduced to nothing more than a pill—as if all his problems lay in more or less dosage. Perhaps, Tony is taking the medicine prescribed and this situation is making him feel personally violated.

Maybe, Tony has gone off the medication with his doctor's best wishes and guidance. His coping with the change is not for others to understand. They should be supportive and only interject when invited.

In this curious, invasive world, we should all take some time to follow etiquette. Instead of prying, be simply loving. You may find your Super Hero friend opening up at a crucial time since you respected him/her over the course of time. "Treat people as they want to be treated."

In addition, be transparent at the right time yourself. Working together, we can help people with disabilities to be cherished for who they are— Super Heroes.

Conclusion:

"Don't be selfish; don't try to impress others. Be humble, thinking of others as better than yourselves. Don't look out only for your own interests, but take an interest in others, too." (Philippians 2:3-4)

Value people for who they are and let them keep their confidentiality confidential.

The Super Hero Manual:
Chapter 8: The "Hideout"

Abstract:

It is essential for the Super Hero to have a safe haven to drop-in on where he/she feels secure enough to take off his/her mask.

Introduction:

The saying goes "Home is where you hang your heart." Many Super Heroes have no conventional homes, but find rest only at their "hideout." This study looks at four elements of a suitable "hideout" for today's Super Hero.

Body:

Element #1:

A satisfactory "hideout" must be welcoming enough for a Super Hero to be able to let his/her hair down. The overall environment of the "hideout" must accommodate a Super Hero's one-of-a-kind traits while still establishing an

36

expectation for behavior that is becoming of society at large.

This tricky equation is accomplished by a team of certified peer support specialists and the painful, yet helpful brushes against other Super Heroes in the "hideout." Yes, relations at times in the 'hideout" can be abrasive, but that is part of Super Hero development.

Element #2:

Super Heroes need to hear the truth from other Super Heroes. What better way to accomplish this then at a Super Heroes' "Hideout." Super Heroes are special and have wisdom in fields of Super Hero powers, temperaments, medications, and other fields. Sometimes to make the truth sink in it takes one Super Hero to enter the same wavelength of thinking as another Super Hero.

Element #3:

In a suitable "hideout," Super Heroes feel a sense of camaraderie. In this family-type setting, Super Heroes are loved for who they are. They find people with similar traits and different traits, but what they have in common is the need for one another. Perhaps, some of these Super Heroes hang their head in shame everywhere they go but the "hideout." As an individual the Super Hero learns that his/her differences from others are not only accepted, but in some way contribute to the environment—drawing him/her as a positive alternative to isolation.

Element #4:

The last element of a successful "hideout" in the study today is a "hideout" that helps the Super Hero find independence or greater independence through finding resources. While a "hideout" builds friendships and is beneficial for the Super Hero demeanor, a "hideout" is only awesome if it points the Super Hero towards standing on his/her own feet.

A 'hideout" should therefore contain groups led by other Super Heroes facilitating lessons that lead the Super Hero in the direction towards a longer life, a suitable place of residence, the ending of bad habits, the fostering of positive habits such as arts and working on spirituality, and just being a more fine-tuned Super Hero.

These life-lessons are learned well on a one-on-one basis as well through mentoring. Mentoring can take place in the most unlikely of places, such as during the transportation of Super Heroes to medical specialists or while playing pool.

Conclusion:

Everyone needs a "home base." Super Heroes need a "hideout" because after they run their homeruns, they tend to burn many bridges if not all of them. Super Heroes need a place they can turn to and for them that tends to be a peer-run safe haven that can be turned to whenever the need strikes. If you have no place to belong to and are a Super Hero, seek another Super Hero to find the "hideout" nearest you.

The Super Hero Manual

Chapter 9: Even Super Heroes Sleep

Abstract:

This study looks at how faith and discipline go hand in hand for successful sleeping as a Super Hero.

Hypothesis:

A regular routine of 8 hours a night at the same time each night is ideal for the sensitive sleeper. This study will consult a Super Hero who specializes in the art of a good night sleep.

Case Study:

Today we will look at the sleep and philosophy of sleep of Mr. A—a Super Hero who sleeps with balance. Although he did not always get the ideal 8-9 hours a night of sleep, Mr. A has been intentional about productive rest for quite some time.

When he was without an official residence to sleep in, Mr. A still knew the secret of not worrying. He "looked" at a "difficult situation" as "temporary"--- that there's hope. Mr. A. recommends not worrying about tomorrow's resources, but rather "peace, tranquility and serenity." He believes that being thankful promotes rest.

During his period of being out of a residence, Mr. A. went to bed for 6-7 hours a night.

Now, he follows a strict regime of no coffee after 2pm and no eating after 7pm. To help him take his super power medication, Mr. A. consumes non-dairy milk to clean out the stomach.

Mr. A. also recommends laying in a flat position before going to bed. In addition, he suggests breathing in your nose, out your mouth. Of significant importance to Mr. A, is a belief in Metaphysics coupled with a fervent faith in God. He believes gems have natural healing qualities.

He recommends that all Super Heroes who have no home seek out a shelter. With his strong faith and constitution Mr. A gives the following charge: "Do not worry about tomorrow." "Tomorrow's not promised."

Conclusion:

With good discipline and sound advice any Super Hero can improve their sleep duration and quality.

The Super Hero Manual

Chapter 10: Occupational Hazards

Abstract:

The Super Hero is recruited for assignment when he/she least expects it. The challenges of the career are unimaginable and the potential for Super Hero professional development are astounding.

Body:

What sets the Super Hero livelihood apart from other professions is the typical truth that the Super Hero never signed a contract nor had a chance to negotiate any of the stipulations of his/her work.

The rigors of the assignment may have come on even at the age of two.

Seems unfair, right?

Super Hero recruitment comes on the spot, at any point in life. It may be brought on by extreme pressure, stress, or have a genetic component.

What is certain is that the Super Hero is needed and that by all means he/she should never give up. There are times to rest. There are times to play. There are times to work, but at all times a Super Hero never ceases to be a Super Hero.

He/she plays a role in helping to save the world. The Super Hero should never quit Assignment Planet Earth until his/her time is up.

If the Super Hero had not experienced certain difficulties, he/she would not have the same gift of empathy. "It takes one to know one" and even now I attest that I have been there.

Conclusion:

Don't give up. Find a Super Hero who can relate at your nearest "Hideout." We are on the same team. With great weakness comes great strength. All of you matter to me, to other Super Heroes, to society, and to God.

Thank you.

The Super Hero Manual

Chapter 11: Conversion Types

Abstract:

1. What is it like to go from 0 – 60 in 3 seconds and then have your metaphorical car wrecked?
2. What is it like to be wrecked and have a stranger fix your "car?"

Body:

Every Super Hero goes through a conversion to super powers experience. Who they turn to during this conversion is important. All that is certain is that it is a rough ride that no one but God can completely understand since each experience is unique. After the Super Hero's conversion experience to the world of disability and one-of-a-kind power(s), they typically go on a Retreat. This expensive vacation is hard for the outside world to understand.

Where has Mr. Energy Plus been for the last three months? Why is he not being a leader like a champ? He has let people down.

Be patient with him/her. (As in put yourself in his/her shoes since he/she is in fact a patient.) It takes some time for the specialists at the Retreat to find the correct balance of Energy, Rest, Relaxation, and Stability. Even after the Retreat's over, expect the Super Hero to need some more rest.

Welcome to the World of misunderstood Super Heroes and Sly Villains. In the movie Spiderman, the grandfather told Peter Parker, "With great power comes great responsibility." This saying resonates truly for the Super Hero and Sly Villain alike. They have both great powers and great weaknesses too. Should they be hasty with their gifts, they will let many people down.

Spider Man saw his family being attacked by the Villain in the story. That was one of the prices he seemed to have to pay. Whether or not you are a Super Hero, you have to pay a price to live out your purpose. It could be running through the pain, smiling in the rain and homelessness, loving when hated and being misunderstood, being accused because of unjust profiling. These things happen regularly to Super Heroes of all shapes and sizes.

The only one who can take care of the situation is Jesus Christ. Jesus stuck to his mission. He never let up. Jesus Christ went through the ultimate conversion experience, but never had the breakdown. He stayed strong and endured it all because of love for mankind, for Super Heroes, for Sly Villains. Jesus cared for them all.

I am glad that God gave me the opportunity to have a second conversion experience to spirituality. Shortly, after June 9th, 1999, I had a conversion experience to disability. There were signs leading up to it, but this was my first full breakdown. I am thankful beyond words that my identity is not wrapped up in my first conversion experience.

People may tell you that converting to life with Jesus is actually insane. These same type of people accused the God of the Universe of being demon possessed. Jesus Christ went through all that for us.

Yes, weaknesses continue, but converting to a lifestyle of discipleship establishes a new identity in Super Heroes, in Sly Villains, in all people. Individuals do not have to carry around the reality of what people label them. Instead, they can say, "I choose to be a Christ-follower. I am saved. I'm living with a new purpose."

Super Heroes do not lose their powers when they convert to a life following Jesus. In fact, they find strength. "Those that wait on the Lord shall renew their strength. They shall mount up with wings like eagles. They shall run and not be weary. They shall walk and not be faint." (Isaiah 40:31)

The only guaranteed effect of conversion to being a Christ-follower is new life. With this new life comes a sound mind, "For God did not give us a spirit of fear, but of power, of love and of a sound mind.' (2 Timothy 1:7)

Yes, there will be continued suffering, but over the horizon will be eternal life.. "I have fought the good fight, I have finished the race, and I have remained faithful. And now the prize awaits me—the crown of righteousness, which the Lord, the righteous Judge, will give me on the day of his return. And the prize is not just for me but for all who eagerly look forward to his appearing." (2 Timothy 4:8)

Conclusion:

The conversion to the super power sickness is painful and requires patience to understand. In this life, another conversion experience is available, conversion to a purposeful life following Jesus.

The Super Hero Manual

Chapter 12: The Elusive "Batmobile"

Abstract:

Full speed ahead and no looking back—The Super Hero travels as quickly as possible, but seldom has a vehicle. He/she has to adapt to the rigors of his environment and at times has to travel great distances to accomplish his/her mission.

Introduction:

What is important in life to a Super Hero who follows the creed: Serve Jesus primarily, Serve humankind secondarily, and Serve Self last? He/she must always remember to still take care of himself/herself. Without a vehicle, it is easy to run ragged on sheer foot power. In this saga, the Super Hero desires the transportation of other Super Heroes and good citizens in order to complete the daily mission.

Body:

Meet Monsieur M. He does his best to reach out as a Super Hero peer support specialist. Sometimes the demands and requests for rides in his "Batmobile" can seem overwhelming. Like his own complex human body system, Monsieur M.'s vehicle requires constant care. Recently, the "Batmobile" required a new battery and as it charged, people everywhere around the "Hideout" admired those wheels of beauty that they did not have.

While many Super Heroes take the public bus system, some need almost completely private transportation. This system of transportation costs a little more, but offers the benefits of being dropped off at specific locations.

Conclusion:

The Super Hero should not be afraid to ask others for help with transportation. The fellowship of the saints, as well as family fellowship, is an important part of the life of the heroic Super Hero and often requires a ride. Whatever distance the Super Hero must go by train, foot, bus, car, to be victorious, he/she will.

The Super Hero Manual

Chapter 13: Abnormally Mortal?

Abstract:

Looking at the standard of Jesus Christ, all mortals that have existed and will exist, exhibit a certain degree of spiritual abnormality in comparison to Him. (Philippians 2:6-8). Yet, even Jesus lived the life of mortality in the body, without sinning. Therefore, it is the thesis of this study that strengths and weaknesses (abnormalities and disabilities) in the body should be considered normal because everyone including Jesus had them.

Introduction:

In the case of the human being, these Super Hero infirmities should be embraced instead of fixed. They should be adapted to instead of ridiculed. These differences between humans can actually be used to bring glory to God and draw others to His face.

Fictional Case Study:

Welcome to the Zone of Light, where there is no fright. People know what to expect. This is the next step in the evolutionary process. Only the same will survive or will they? It is the age of well-toned cloning. Not a sickness in sight. There are no Super Heroes since nobody needs them.

Everyone is self-sufficient in his/her own little biosphere. There are plenty of planets to go around and these humans have been to them all. This is truly the American Dream!

Truthful Case Study of Jesus Christ:

"You must have the same attitude that Christ Jesus had. Though he was God, he did not think of equality with God as something to cling to. Instead, he gave up his divine privileges; he took the humble position of a slave and was born as a human being. When he appeared in human form, he humbled himself in obedience to God and died a criminal's death on a cross. Therefore, God elevated him to the place of highest honor and gave him the name above all other names, that at the name of Jesus every knee should bow, in heaven and on earth and under the earth, and every tongue confess that Jesus Christ is Lord, to the glory of God the Father." (Philippians 2:5-11)

Body:

We need each other, just as we need Jesus Christ. If someone were to lose a leg in God's Family, would they survive? Yes! A key in the process for survival is not what we have as individuals, but who we are collectively. We do not need to pretend we have perfect bodies. We must humble ourselves by being honest about the needs we have. On the contrary to hoarding what talents we have for survival, we must pour ourselves into other people and let them pour back into us. Jesus gave His all and He is elevated to the "place of highest honor."

Jesus demonstrated that the "last shall be first and the first shall be last." We must emulate this theme and hold brothers and sisters in high esteem who seem to be the most broken. This will build us all up.

Together, we can beat the evolutionary food chain and apart, everyone will die—even the supposed upper tier "perfect" people.

Conclusion:

I need you and you need me. We all need each other and all have different strengths and weaknesses.

The Super Hero Manual

Chapter 14: The Epic Vision

Abstract:

Dreams are dreamed and then dreams are made. During the conversion to psychosis process, "ordinary" people are converted into Super Heroes with great potential. This potential is ignited by goals of epic proportions.

Introduction:

Making a great impact on this earth involves:

(1) Knowing the power of God in us. (Philippians 4:13, 2 Timothy I :7)
(2) Knowing that we have great potential as vision is spoken into us (by anyone, particularly brethren and the Lord). (Proverbs 29:18)
(3) Setting goals and strategically working to meet them with obedience to God as the top priority. (Psalms 37:4)
(4) Trusting the Lord when things do not seem to go as planned. (Proverbs 3:5-6)

Body:

Element #1:

It is He who created us. He birthed us with a vision of greatness. We were made to glorify the Lord! His power is real and evident in us. We must simply capture the truth of who we are in Christ.

"I can do all things through Christ who strengthens me." (Philippians 4:13)

"For God did not give us a spirit of fear, but of power, of love, and of a sound mind." (2 Timothy 1:7)

Since we can do all things, it's time to gain vision of what we're supposed to do.

Element #2:

"Where there is no vision, the people perish: but he that keepeth the law, happy is he." (Proverbs 29:18)

We realize that as potential is spoken over us, through prayer and others, we need to run with it. We should piece together dreams, visions, prayers, the words of others into an action plan called purpose. For we were made for greatness!

Element #3:

"Delight thyself also in the LORD: and he shall give thee the desires of thine heart." (Psalm 37:4) As we develop an action plan, we need to be sure to make God the focus. When we glorify God in what we aspire to be, He gives us our deepest desires. This includes the desire to make an impact on the Kingdom of God with our unique chemical make-up and gifts.

Taking the time to intentionally make goals and set out how they will be achieved for the glory of God brings fulfillment. Thus the Super Hero's role fits neatly in like a puzzle piece for the good of everyone.

Element #4:

"Trust in the Lord with all your heart. Lean not on your own understanding. In all your ways acknowledge Him and He shall direct your paths." (Proverbs 3:5-6)

Dreams do not typically come true in a day. A refinement process is necessary to chisel Super Power strengths. The journey is not easy but it is well worth it. Joseph, The Dreamer, experienced these growth pains as his grandiose dreams came to fruition. In the end, as he honored God even in prison, he was given a much elevated political position.

Super Heroes frequently have mind hiccups and periods of brain flatulence. They make enormous mistakes and have to bounce back. However, the mission is not a failure until the Hero quits. Run like the wind friends and put your trust in Jesus!

Conclusion:

Super Heroes are super because of the God-given talent Lucifer has tried to destroy. Do not give up. Set a goal with your vision and continue to the end of the race to the glory of God. Hallelujah.

The Super Hero Manual

Chapter 15: Headlines and Shadows

Preface:

First and foremost, before this chapter begins, it is necessary to declare that the true leader inside every Super Hero is Jesus. He is the model of love and purpose. Christ lived on this earth sacrificially. Although he eventually made the headlines like no other, Jesus gave all glory to God.

Abstract:

Modeling after Christ, the true Super Hero seeks to become less by living in such a way to bring fame to God. He/she may do spectacular feats without being recognized on this earth. Of course the Super Hero is a mere mortal and at times of weakness and peril, especially mental illness, he/she has a tendency to go against this creed. To run against this tendency, despite all the resistance, is a mark of true heroics.

Fictitious Case Study:

Look up, Look high. It's Cray Man to the scene rescuing another piece of litter from rain gutters of Mulberry Pies Building. To this point, Cray Man has seemed like a true hero, picking trash up everywhere to the glory of God. Today, Cray Man will have to swim out of this headline-rich scene. He finds himself cleaning in the midst of Twichpic County Parade.

Headline: Cray "Z" Man Breaks Gutter and Falls Through Window At Twichpic County Parade

By Conscientious Observer

(Fictitious)

It was glorious weather for a County Parade. The birds were in town. Mulberry was baking her famous pies. This was to be the weekend focusing on Mayor Trindle's Inauguration. Unfortunately, Twichpic County came to known a different showstopper—that ironically enough a man who was known to take the background and lovingly nicknamed "Cray Man." His days as a fish in water are unofficially over, as today he made the scene by foolishly destroying national landmark property. People could be heard from the crowd, Chanting, "Crrra, Crrra, Crrrazy Man." What a fool. We'll always love him.

Conclusion:

It is unfortunate that once a Super Hero makes the headlines, a great amount of pressure is placed on him/her. His/her reputation is never the same again and frequently he/she may retreat to the "hideout" to cope. That does not mean that his/her hero days are over by any means. For the true Super Hero knows that God recognizes him/her for who he/she is today, not yesterday. It's about serving Christ all the time, whether in the background or center stage.

The Super Hero Manual

Chapter 16: Keep Your Day Job?

What constitutes a career, hobby, or recreation?

What constitutes a consistent successful Super Hero?

Fictional Case Study:

1.

The alarm system stood faithful on the wall, still doing its job after years of service.

Tony, sitting in a pile of drool, an unfortunate side-effect of one of his medications, reminisces of how he had thought the machinery for the alarm up. His Super Hero ingenuity had been planted in hundreds of thousands of homes, saving innumerable lives. Tony, who now lives his life on disability, feels a sense of accomplishment and gratitude to God despite his late onset frequently occurring seizures.

2.

And then there's Jessica. She began life with dreams of becoming a Broadway songstress. Along the way, with all the excitement of college musicals and the loss of her father, Jessica developed a severe case of Bipolar. She was hospitalized her after she burnt half of her hair off. Now, Jessica sings solos once a year at her church Christmas Music event. It brings her much fulfillment.

Tony with his frequent seizures and recently hospitalized Jessica, with her Bipolar Disorder, are not living what many consider the American Dream. Their lives seem frazzled and half-lived, but they know they are not here to make an impression on you! Jesus Christ rules their lives and they know that in His eyes, they are the same Super Hero that they dreamed of becoming at 5 years of age. Forget the status quo. A life lived for Jesus is a life lived to fulfillment—no matter the dollar sign.

You can take away the money, the world's definition of occupation. Now, what makes a man/woman? It's his/her relationship with Jesus and secondarily, the difference he/she makes for the Kingdom of God.

You people reading this are pretty awesome. Don't let anyone tell you the difference you can make in this world. This is a temporary world needing everyone to love intentionally with the after-life in mind.

You may lead a soul to Christ. You may keep a friend from suicide. You may keep someone from committing murder. You may not even be aware of what you have done, but God knows.

"Man looks on the outward appearance, but God looks on the heart."

Consider a career in loving like Jesus. All it takes is everything you have to offer.

The Super Hero Manual

Chapter 17: Insanity Gone Hip

To American Society:

So re-package me and make me into what you want me to be "Cruel World."

Do I look like a beer on energy to you? Call me "LOCO."

Are you too beautiful? Is that why Backstreet Boys declares that you "drive" them "crazy?"

Wait, you mean to tell me that you didn't trick these young ladies into taking their clothes off for the camera? You are telling me that they are just plain "Gone Wild?"

What is "wild?" What is "crazy?" What is "loco?" What is respect?

Do you think this extreme terminology is fair game to make money off of or do its derivatives poke fun at real people?
Maybe if you drink enough of your special beverage, you can go through a period of psychosis too.

Does that sound like an advertisement? America, land of the free, why do you allow me to be exploited through your commercialism?

Where is the decency? What is Popular Culture except to mean barbaric mob mentality?

It's the same relentless follow the crowd that nailed Jesus to the cross as they shouted, Crucify Him. Crucify Him."

It's the same attitude that tolerates Abortion.

This is American Pop Culture. I am here to stay and not everyone will agree, but forever will it remain, that "the road to life is narrow" and that "few find it." "And the road to destruction is wide and many find it."

The Super Hero Manual

Chapter 18: The Role of Spirituality in Self-Efficacy

Abstract:

God is everything in the life of the Super Hero. Confidence in oneself is only because the Holy Spirit is in oneself. Mary Mary was right when she sang of her accomplishments by singing, "It's the God in me." Similarly, in the following case study, a Super Hero named "Critter" "from Crittendom" shares about how his reliance is found in his Creator.

Case Study:

"I wouldn't be if it wasn't for God. It's not a choice, it's a have to. Anything and everything, I guarantee it. And it's because of God that I am."

Body:

What is it to rely on yourself in the traditional sense of the word, "self-efficacy?"

Does it focus on the ability to attain the next big car, career, wife, family, the white picket fence? What happens when the anchor of success tears loose due to trauma or loss of a loved one? In many lives, the human experience can come tottering down as man struggles to find meaning.

"Critter" acknowledges that every part of him is from God. I believe that God is Critter's stability.

Conclusion:

The Super Hero cannot depend successfully on something flimsy as his/her human experience. However, with God, the consumer can say, "I can do all things through Christ who strengthens me." (Philippians 4:13)   Such faith is spiritual efficacy at its finest.

The Super Hero Manual

Chapter 19: Super Power Obedience Anointing

Fictitious Case Study:

Dr. Jinx thought he could recreate the Sphinx in Egypt with ten workers and loads of concrete. His project was to be built in the mountains of Utah for a museum. After hiring the workers, who purchased expensive equipment to begin, Dr. Jinx decided to break the law and not pay his taxes.

This simple decision created a chain reaction of distrust in new employees who quit after they learned Dr. Jinx was being pursued by the IRS. "But the money was used for a good cause," was all he could manage to say. Too bad for the damaged land on a project not complete. Too bad for employees out of work who invested in equipment. And too bad for Dr. Jinx who was left much poorer than he started.

Body:

Before we take on mountains in this lifetime, we should be faithful with little first. God honors obedience more than sacrifice.

He looks for those Super Heroes as well as "ordinary" heroes who are willing to be set apart for Him. When a person is obedient to Christ in everyday matters, they prepare to stand for the Lord whatever the cost. In times of trying, their spiritual houses will be built upon a rock and stand to pressure.

Super Power Obedience Anointing means that a Super Hero's powers will actually increase as the hero depends on God in everyday obedience. With the discipline of obedience, comes God's power brightly being displayed in the talents already present in the Super Hero and in other abilities he/she did not possess before. The experience is nothing short of miraculous.

Integrity becomes increased trust and blessings. Purity becomes having needs met and being an example. Financial integrity becomes increased opportunities.

Dr. Jinx did not need to build the Sphinx to find significance, he should have patiently paid his taxes and let God meet his desires.

Conclusion:

The obedient Super Hero will submit to God, make requests of God for his/her needs, and anticipate great things.

"We walk by faith not by sight." (2 Corinthians 5:7)

Dare today to take a small step of faith instead of a large fatal step of risky disobedience.

The Super Hero Manual

Chapter 20: Motivation

Abstract:

Super Heroes need more than just the help of other Super Heroes. They need the help of the entire Body of Christ. (This includes Super Heroes and "ordinary" everyday heroes.) "The human body has many parts, but the many parts make up one whole body. So it is with the body of Christ. Some of us are Jews, some are Gentiles, some are slaves, and some are free. But we have all been baptized into one body by one Spirit, and we all share the same Spirit (1 Corinthians 12:12-13)."

Introduction:

Captain Planet had a great concept when he said, "By your powers combined, I'm Captain Planet." For what can a part of the Body do isolated? We need each other, just as the eye needs the nose, and the ears need the toes.

In fact, it took a small section of the Body of Christ at a local church to come together in unison to pray over me that I would have the motivation to write this chapter today. With the support of others in the Body of Christ, motivational power from God came on me strong and I immediately put the pen to paper after a period of failed attempts.

"But our bodies have many parts, and God has put each part just where he wants it. How strange a body would be if it had only one part! Yes, there are many parts, but only one body. The eye can never say to the hand, "I don't need you." The head can't say to the feet, "I don't need you." In fact, some parts of the body that seem weakest and least important are actually the most necessary. And the parts we regard as less honorable are those we clothe with the greatest care (1 Corinthians 12:18-23)."

Yes, it is impossible to stay motivated standing on a rock far away, alone. If we call upon the Lord God, He will help. Frequently, this help comes through other members of the Body.

You may think from time to time that some of these heroes are not heroes at all. They may appear to be spying and hypocritical Sly Villains rather than helpers in the Body. However, is not God the Judge of who in the end will be a Sly Villain or a Super Hero? Everyone on this earth has a chance and may need motivation to become a Christ-follower too.

Body:

To stay motivated as a Super Hero, ask for help. First, call upon the Lord your God who will not let you be "put to shame." Second, accept the help He provides in the form of others.

Third, be strategic. Develop a plan! Seek help from God and others in this plan. Make sure you take a Sabbath day once a week at the very least. This is mandatory for both Super Heroes and "ordinary" heroes. For God orchestrated it for our benefit.

To build momentum, work on your project every day except your Sabbath Day. Tell others about your project in order to be motivated further. Tell God about it and don't be legalistic (set in stone) about your schedule.

If emergencies come up, take a day or two off. If a mental health emergency comes up, take off as much time as necessary.

Conclusion:

Remember, by combining the forces of the Church Body together, under the direction of Christ, mountains are moved. We need each other and we need you! Do not give up. Be motivated through God's power to be who you are made to be.

Chapter 21: Freedom Song

Abstract:

"Comfort, comfort my people,"says your God. "Speak tenderly to Jerusalem. Tell her that her sad days are gone and her sins are pardoned. Yes, the LORD has punished her twice over for all her sins." Listen! It's the voice of someone shouting, "Clear the way through the wilderness for the LORD! Make a straight highway through the wasteland for our God!" (Isaiah 40:1-3)

Who we are today, does not have to be the same as we were yesterday! This is a happy, joyous day.

Case Study:

Senor Brad had a mental breakdown about ten years. From time to time, people remind him of his previous diagnosis of Bipolar. They call him crazy and stupid, completely not understanding him. What they don't understand is that Senor Brad is a Super Hero now. Years ago, he was diagnosed, but now he is a genuine hero who made a conversion not just to psychosis, but to God. Ever since, Brad has not been the same.

Body:

"This means that anyone who belongs to Christ has become a new person. The old life is gone; a new life has begun!" (2 Corinthians 5:17)

Senor Brad has experienced the saving grace of Jesus Christ! Nothing can take that away from him, not a loss of sanity, not extreme poverty, not any loss in this world. If Senor Brad is a new creation and the old is gone, then Senor Brad has a new identity. Thus, he can walk in power as a true Super Hero by the move of the Holy Spirit. The past is over.

Conclusion:

"I waited patiently for the LORD to help me, and he turned to me and heard my cry. He lifted me out of the pit of despair, out of the mud and the mire. He set my feet on solid ground and steadied me as I walked along. He has given me a new song to sing a hymn of praise to our God.
Many will see what he has done and be amazed. They will put their trust in the LORD."

(Psalms 40:1-3)

Call on Jesus, He will hear your cry, and pull you out of the muck.

Chapter 22: The Big Game

75

Introduction:

Now rallying champions! This is it. This is the Big Dance before Angelic Audiences. The game is a foot. But this isn't a game. This is life and death.

You think you got skills? What are skills in the Kingdom of Heaven?

This is where it all goes down. Ball's in your court. Jesus has given you the pass. You have options: Be a show-off. Pass to your teammate. Walk up and dribble.

What should you do? Clock-ticking… You are surrounded by such a great cloud of witnesses. You can sneak an elbow and be perfectly set up in the zone. You can play by the rules and risk it all.

You choose to go for a three-pointer. You are so on the Jesus Team. You are the Big-Shot Star you sink it, time runs out. Jesus Team wins.

Woohoo! This is it.

"Get away from me. You may wear the jersey, but you were never on my team."

Huh?

Truth Huddle:

Not everyone who calls out to me, 'Lord! Lord!'
will enter the Kingdom of Heaven. Only those who
actually do the will of my Father in heaven will
enter. [22] On judgment day many will say to me,
'Lord! Lord! We prophesied in your name and cast
out demons in your name and performed many
miracles in your name.' [23] But I will reply, 'I never
knew you. Get away from me, you who break
God's laws.' (Matthew 7:21-23)

"What did I do wrong?"

Personal Case Study:

I, Daniel, am writing to you today about my fate, if
I so choose. I am in the game and I have been for
some time, but if I do not enter the sheepfold
Christ's way, I am nothing. If I do not live my life
with the love of God, I am nothing. If it seems that
I even do miracles, but have not love, I am
nothing.

Love is laying down my life for the cause of love.
Jesus is love. The rules to the game called life are
out of this world. They do not seem natural. It is
so much more than putting a ball in the hoop at the
right time. It is infinitely more than being a star.

Depending on who you are in the Body of Christ,
playing basketball in the game of life might be
being the Golden Water Person, being a referee,

being a star player who gives all glory to God because he/she himself//herself has no talent in his/her own strength.

Being successful is more about making Jesus a star than anything else. It is about showing off to Him for His glory. Yes, there is a great cloud of witnesses cheering us on, but selfish gain will be nowhere to be found.

The Super Hero Manual

Chapter 23: Secret Missions, Real Missions

Humble Beginnings:

Every great man/woman begins life as a helpless infant dependent on a caretaker and God Himself.

Real Living:

Jesus began life on earth as a babe and rose up to be a great shepherd of many men and women. We have the potential to live great lives as shepherds and shepherdesses if we simply live as Jesus lived.

Secret Missions:

The devil himself would like to lead all mankind (including Super Heroes) on a secret mission to their death.

Why?

Super Heroes have potential. All people have potential. And pride was the downfall of the devil when he converted his powers to evil purposes.

The devil would like to tempt all of us with potential into prideful psychosis. It starts with taking on too much—trying to be a Super Hero without the motivation of the Holy Spirit—nor the Body of Christ.

Real Mission:

Our mission is to love. We need to love God and love people. Working together, we need to keep each other in check because we are not Jesus. We cannot accomplish anything by our own strength. Doing the dishes and forgiveness are examples of love in action. This mission will not always be seen by others, but it will make the profound impact necessary to collectively change the world.

Conclusion:

Look to Jesus, our Shepherd to learn to love mankind. Avoid secret missions that pridefully isolate the Super Hero from other heroes.

The Super Hero Manual

Chapter 24: Cancer Kills

Right to the Source:

Wake up America. People are dying. There's an illness that's going around and it's genetic. It feeds on human flesh and eats people alive. It spreads from within. Foreign contaminants can trigger this condition. It is as common as the human condition. When it is fully grown, it gives birth to death.

Body:

"But every man is tempted, when he is drawn away of his own lust, and enticed. Then when lust hath conceived, it bringeth forth sin: and sin, when it is finished, bringeth forth death."   (James 1:14-15)

We are the Body of Christ—Super Heroes and Ordinary Heroes. If one part of the Body has cancer, we must care. If the sin cancer should spread, the entire Body could be in jeopardy.

" Your boasting about this is terrible. Don't you realize that this sin is like a little yeast that spreads through the whole batch of dough? Get rid of the old "yeast" by removing this wicked person from among you. Then you will be like a fresh batch of dough made without yeast, which is what you really are. Christ, our Passover Lamb, has been sacrificed for us. So let us celebrate the festival, not with the old breadof wickedness and evil, but with the new bread of sincerity and truth.

When I wrote to you before, I told you not to associate with people who indulge in sexual sin. But I wasn't talking about unbelievers who indulge in sexual sin, or are greedy, or cheat people, or worship idols. You would have to leave this world to avoid people like that. I meant that you are not to associate with anyone who claims to be a believer yet indulges in sexual sin, or is greedy, or worships idols, or is abusive, or is a drunkard, or cheats people. Don't even eat with such people.

[12] It isn't my responsibility to judge outsiders, but it certainly is your responsibility to judge those inside the church who are sinning."

(1 Corinthians 5:6-12)

Remove the cancer? Would not that be mean?

Respect for Christ's Church (Body of Christ) is extremely important. It must be taken care of like a human body and if any part rebels against survival, it must be cut off.

Praise the Lord for restoration and forgiveness— that "Man looks on the outward appearance, but God looks on the heart." Christ is my final judge and the final judge of any Super Hero.

Conclusion:

Do not let the cancer of sin in your life. Cut it out at all costs.

The Super Hero Manual

Chapter 25: "Bad Dog"

AIM:

To Point out Satan for who he is.

BODY:

I had a dream in the middle of the night. I was like a soldier gone to battle. These strange organic animal-like objects started appearing bent on one thing—my destruction. As they appeared to mutilate me one turned into what appeared to be a simple mutt. I thought, yeah, let's tame this little one. Let's domesticate it.

But when I tried to feed it dog food, it refused. It wanted to feed on my flesh. It waited rather impatiently while I prepared to go through the army's ration supplies. I said, "Good dog! You are being a good dog!" The dog smiled and continued to wait rather impatiently.

As I awoke, I realized that this dog related to my life. The dog represented Satan who would be happy to pretend to be pacified. He would be glad for me to assume he has a two year old mind.

God knows the best thing to do with him and his minions are to command them to flee and then to destroy them in the lake of fire. There's no entertaining this creature. There's no catering to his needs.

This bad dog has got to be put down in our lives or he will eat the children of the promise.

We cannot do it on our own. Otherwise, Satan will deceive us. We need to know the foe we are facing. We need to know that Satan is not some puppy dog we can turn to our liking.

Conclusion:

"The thief comes to steal, kill, and destroy, but I (Jesus) come that they might have life and that more abundantly."

We must stand in power with Jesus and know our foe. Otherwise, "the cares of this world" are going to topple us.

The Super Hero Manual

Chapter 26: Memorial Stones

Introduction:

It was the hour I changed—the hour I became someone new. Memorials are memories. Before, you could call me disabled. Before, you could call me burdened. Yet, at this transition, there was a "shift in the atmosphere." Personal Revival had birthed in me. I would "never be the same again."

Body:

When a Super Hero is suffering, it is powerful and essential to look back at those Memorial Stones marking who he/she really is. Some people have Super Powers, but few are Super Heroes. Few have had birthed inside them a force so strong that it leads them to do the otherwise impossible, rooted in love.

My Memorial Stone was set in place the same way other Memorials are set in place—through death. Someone had to die. That someone was Jesus. The Memorial was my Baptism—December 31st, 2011. When I went under the water and returned to air, an obedient change came over me. I have not always lived it, but a seed died that day. This was a seed that God can work with in my life to this day. The Bible says in Acts 2:37-38, "Repent and be baptized in the name of Jesus for the remission of sins and the Holy Spirit will come upon you." Today is a new beginning for me. I look back at that Memorial Stone and remember the Holy Spirit has created in me a disdain for sin and a love of abundant living. If any force on this earth tries to steer me wrong, I will remember that I was baptized with Jesus Christ Himself and I have much reason to move forward.

Conclusion:

Greatness lies in the most unlikely of places. Do not underestimate others and do not underestimate the power of God working in you. ~Daniel K. Arnold

parablesoftoday@gmail.com

BOOK II

Ever-Changing:

A Super Hero Manual Book

by

Daniel K. Arnold

Ever-Changing: A Super Hero Manual Book:
Table of Contents

Ever-Changing:

A Super Hero Manual Book

Chapter 1: Introduction

I am a Super Hero. Not every day seems epic.
Regardless, I seek to live my days for God.

A Super Hero is a person who lives supernaturally
for Jesus, despite the realities of a disability.
Super Heroes have the power to change the world.
Some days feel phenomenal, some days are
ordinary, and some days substandard. However,
coping by the power of God, to be the best one can
be, is epic.

Isaiah 40:30-31

"Even youths grow tired and weary, and young
men stumble and fall; but those who hope in the
LORD will renew their strength. They will soar on
wings like eagles; they will run and not grow
weary, they will walk and not be faint."

<u>Ever-Changing:</u>

<u>A Super Hero Manual Book</u>

Chapter 2: Mister Energy Plus

In <u>The Super Hero Manual</u>, Mister Energy Plus was seen on the cover. The explanation of the cover was segmented. Chapter 2 and Chapter 3 serve to flesh out the persona of Mister Energy Plus and his extra persona, "Black Bird Ops." The purpose of these two chapters is to case study a specific Super Hero type (mental disability coupled with spirituality) and demonstrate his/her capacity to glorify God.

Case Study:

Mister Energy Plus fits the archetype of the modern Type 2 Bipolar Disorder. He has moments of excessive energy as well as diminished energy. His rocket feet show his predicament of not being able to contain his momentum on his own. The blue bands encompassing his body demonstrate that he is functioning under a containment system. His belt shows that he is positively charged. His battery backpack contains two negative charged symbols showing that the Lithium charge balances out his excessive positive charge. The sun symbolizes his potential for pride and the Bible is held out in front of the sun to help him focus and calibrate with what's important. Theory is without these coping mechanisms, Mister Energy Plus, aka Daniel K. Arnold, would fly to the sun and burn up.

Theory:

Mister Energy Plus is coping, but has not always been. Many times he's glorified God with writing and leading Bible Study, but at other times he has spun out of control. He is far from perfect, but still manages to live an exciting life. He would not have it any other way.

Conclusion:

Take one day at a time. Be who you are meant to be. Cope with God's help and the resources God has put on this earth. "On hearing this, Jesus said, "It is not the healthy who need a doctor, but the sick. But go and learn what this means: 'I desire mercy, not sacrifice.' For I have not come to call the righteous, but sinners (Mark 2:17)."

Ever-Changing:

A Super Hero Manual Book

Chapter 3: Black Bird Ops

Black Bird Ops is a fantasy, yet real persona. Under this guise, Mister Energy Plus feels more significant and at the same time is more on edge. He becomes more aware of every sound and stimuli around him.

With a black mask on, he hides in the shadows and works to fight crime in his own way. Still wearing the lithium backpack, every bit of his uniform is stained in black for   cover-up.

He holds a smaller Bible than before, with a cross on the center and acts rather seriously. He carries a pair of noids on either side of his shoulders and Abilify implants around his legs with the term Ability to represent the debilitation of the medication Abilify.

Schizoaffective is the world's stigma for Black Bird Ops.

Reality:

Sometimes Mister Energy Plus arises. Sometimes Black Bird Ops arises.

Is this a reality any Super Hero can face? David said in the Psalms, "With my God I can scale a wall (2 Samuel 22:30)."

Conclusion:

It's hard to face myself sometimes. This is an aspect of who I can be. I must rely on God to pick me up and salvage what's left of me. I need not hide behind a mask, but I cannot reveal everything to the world.

This is my predicament. This is my life. I've burned many bridges, but my real friends have stuck by me. It has been said that I am misunderstood.

As we do not have to live with sin, we do not have to live with our present condition. By faith, we can be ever changing from glory to glory. Even as our bodies decay, our minds can renew. Black Bird Ops, you do not have to stay.

"Do not conform to the pattern of this world, but be transformed by the renewing of your mind. Then you will be able to test and approve what God's will is--his good, pleasing and perfect will (Romans 12:2)."

I am unique. I am one-of-a-kind. My body is not perfect. Once again, I quote my Mom: "God made you and God made no junk."

Ever-Changing:

A Super Hero Manual Book

Chapter 4: New Day

I like when the sun comes out after a storm. *"**As far as the east is from the west,** so far has he* removed our transgressions from us (Psalms 103:12)."

Yesterday can be truly over.

And when we begin a new moment, what do we think about?

It is certainly a great time to tune into the voice of God—a tune never regretted.

When God speaks those quiet unctions, man is changed, encouraged, transformed by the power of the Holy Ghost. I have had some God experiences that are out of this world.

"We walk by faith not by sight   (2 Corinthians 5:7)."

"What do you want God to do for you?" (I heard a pastor say.)

I say dwell with me. Empower me to live a holy life. Put the right people around me. Bless my comings and my goings. Anything is possible with God. Do you really believe that?

Experience the anointing of the Lord God today!

"But the Comforter, which is the Holy Ghost, whom the Father will send in my name, He will teach you all things and bring all things to your remembrance—whatsoever I have said unto you (John 14:26)."

Do you know Jesus Lord supernaturally?

Has God spoken to you and blessed you with the gifts of the Holy Spirit?

He is real.

Pursue Him and He will give you understanding.

Ever-Changing:

A Super Hero Manual Book

Chapter 5: Deeper

I am not always sure of what to say or what to do. At moments like this, I tune into the voice of God.

I seek out confirmation of this voice and know that He will "never leave" me "nor forsake" me. He will speak and oh so clearly. He is ever-present and all-knowing. He truly cares.

Rest.

Let Him have control.

Let all fear subside.

Jesus is Lord!

The Super Hero and anyone can enter into bliss in the Lord. Dwelling with God is powerful as all distractions subside. The playing field is equalized as we sit and dine with a holy God who has torn away the separating veil that blocked communication.

Weaknesses become testimonies to draw in the broken.

Strengths are put in God's hands for His glory— "for every good and perfect gift comes from the Father of Lights (James 1:17)."

This is the season of joy and jubilee. This is the time believers come together in one accord.

We come to praise.

We come to rest in Him.

We come to hear God's voice, corporately as well as personally! Our experience is not always perfect; for we have imperfect senses.

One day we will have new bodies in true bliss. Until then, "Let everything that has breath praise the Lord (Psalms 150:7)!"

This is our season of breakthrough.

Chapter 6: "Just Visiting"

The sorrows we encounter in life will not last.
They are temporal. One man loses his child,
another his leg. We are to "mourn with those who
mourn."

In the same light, we should be happy with those
who are happy. There is "a time for every purpose
under Heaven (Ecclesiastes 3:1)."

This chapter is entitled, "Just Visiting" in reference
to suffering. Our home is not on earth, but in
Heaven.

Picture the game "Monopoly." Some passed
through on the narrow portion of the game square
and were "Just Visiting."

Others were actually stuck in jail.

Let us live our lives with an eternal perspective.
Let us have an after-life to be looking forwards to.
Let our sorrows be in a period of "Just Visiting."

We can learn something from suffering and picture
how much Jesus had to pay that we might have
eternal life.

It's time to be thankful for our future, grateful that
we have this life to live, and thankful that God's
changing our hearts for the better.

Next time you play Monopoly, remember that the narrow path is "Just Visiting" sorrow—great things are in store!

Ever-Changing:

A Super Hero Manual Book

Chapter 7: Lull Period

Not every day is meant to be exciting for the Super Hero.

"There is a time and purpose for every season under Heaven (Ecclesiastes 3:1)."

Some moments are for rest.

Some moments are for work.

Some moments are for spiritual recharging.

Recharging does not equate with feeling energetic, but rather balanced.

Like a rollercoaster, an abundance of feel good energy, does not equate with actual energy. The mind can be deceitful. True rest comes to those who spend time communing with God.

How much rest time is necessary is up to the individual hero and his/her Higher Power. Deposits made in the bank of rest with God benefit the hero, but balance is necessary there too.

Sabbath day comes once a week as God rested after six days. Balance is crucial to fulfill responsibilities. Nonetheless, it is a must for the hero to communicate with the God of Universe daily.
Focus is spent at this time. Energy is allocated to revere God and hear from him.

Even music takes time for rest periods. Everyone needs recovery time with God and the Super Hero is no exception.

Ever-Changing:

A Super Hero Manual Book

Chapter 8: Communication

We are on a commission from God. As a unified Body of Christ,
"we are sent."

Although communication with God can involve the corporate Body, I believe it is most intimate on an individual basis. We, the Spirit-filled believers can tap into a realm of communication that is real, unique, clear, wonderful, and best of all, close to God. For the Godhead has entered our very beings.

Consultation with God can become direct in nature.

Nothing else is quite as genuine as hearing from the God within.

Namaste.

I greet the God in you because we are of the same spirit.

I am not referring to idolatry using the term "god", but the God who makes His home inside all true believers.

I am not here to please, but to be an agent of liberty. I am not the solution, but I know who holds it. Rest in the Lord. Be filled. Hold onto the promises of God.

Waahaaha…

Be the person God created you to be.

Do not shy away from being culturally relevant! We are to be "in the world but not of it."

Let "A Whole New World" in this same world captivate you.

This is the world of change. This is the world of being filled. "Delight yourself in the law of the Lord and He shall give you the desires of your heart." (Psalm 37:4) "What do you wish for Aladdin?"

God is no genie. He is actually all-powerful, but He will grant you new life and the desires of your heart if you seek Him with pure motive.

Live the dream life.

Live the free life.

Prosperity is connected with being prosperous. Blessings follow you where you go.

Why?

The Lord lavishes blessings on His children.

"But the Comforter, which is the Holy Ghost, whom the Father will send in my name. He will teach you all things and bring all things to your remembrance—whatsoever I have spoken unto you (John 14:26)."

All things means we will not have lack!

All things means that God is our final authority for wisdom and not mere man.

All things means certain breakthrough.

So "break on through to the other side. Break on through to the other side (Break On Through (To Other Side, The Doors)."

Ask God to open up the line of communication with you today!

Ever-Changing:

A Super Hero Manual Book

Chapter 9: What Do You Want?

Breakthrough happens when Christ's followers open their mouths and ask God for it. "Ye have not because ye ask not (James 4:2)," is not just a saying. It's a promise.

"What do you want out of life?" Christ followers. You took the time to obey God. Now look forwards!

"Delight yourself in the law of the Lord and He will give you the desires of your heart (Psalm 37:4)."

I like the classic song "Jesus On the Mainline." "Just call him up and tell Him what you want (Silvestri)."

What do you want out of life?

Since "all things are possible with God (Matthew 19:26)," it is time to stop settling for consolation. No, we are to "run as to get the prize (1 Corinthians 19:24)."

Case Study #1:

I walked down the street led by the Spirit. I asked for God's lead. When I became frustrated after walking far, I uttered, "God if you are truly leading this, let me run into someone I know."

Within minutes, I ran into a believer's house. "Ask, and it shall be given you; seek, and ye shall

find; knock, and it shall be opened unto you
(Matthew 7:7)."

Case Study #2:

My friend and I walked down M.A.C. Avenue to
evangelize. We were led by the Spirit.
Eventually, I said, "If we are really going to
infiltrate, we need to know someone at a party.
God can do anything." Within minutes, we
approached a party where I knew a person well.

Case Study #3:

I desired for it to stop raining to do street
evangelism. I went on a bus in the late evening
believing it could possibly be not raining in East
Lansing. I inquired on the bus, "Wouldn't it be
amazing if it didn't rain in East Lansing?"

By the time we got to East Lansing, there was no
rain.

Concept:

James 1:5 says, "If any of you lacks wisdom, let
Him ask of God who gives generously without
finding fault, but he must not doubt."

These case studies involved making requests
known verbally by faith.

What do you want out of life?

My Story:

I am a Super Hero—sometimes misunderstood. In my opinion, if I do not shoot for the moon, what's the purpose?

God can do great things in us, but we must not settle for mediocrity.

Conclusion:

We need to ask God by faith for not just what we need, but what we desire.

Then, "Anticipate great things (Brian L. Arnold)."

Ever-Changing:

A Super Hero Manual Book

Chapter 10: Wise Words

Now that we have "freedom" and "confidence" as we approach God, we definitely should let go of unproductive dialogue.

As we approach our fellow man with love and forgiveness, let us be purposeful.

Paul in Ephesians 5, speaks of "always being thankful."

Thanksgiving should come out of our lips, instead of idle words.

Imagine the beauty of a person who shows discernment with his/her lips. If humankind uttered no idle words, wise men would tune in to every last word. To the least of these, we can be like a fresh fountain pouring out insight from the God within us. Shall we mix fresh spring water with a little bit of poisoned drink?

By all means no!

Let us be rather "making the most of every opportunity for the days are evil (Ephesians 5:16)." Let us be taken seriously by even the enemy as well as the allies.

"Submit yourselves therefore to God. Resist the devil, and he will flee from you (James 4:7)." "Clap your hands, all you nations; shout to God with cries of joy (Psalm 47:1)."

Chapter 11: Pride

Puffed up, self-centered, egocentric.

Fictitious Case Study:

Johnny was completely focused on himself. He believed has was "the stuff."

He had a topnotch job, topnotch car and a topnotch girlfriend. He always believed that he could beat the system when he rebelled.

Unfortunately, for his ego, the IRS caught up with him. Due to his pride, he received the maximum sentence.

"Pride goes before destruction, a haughty spirit before a fall (Proverbs 16:18)." Super Heroes may have a heightened level of pride while in a state of mania.

This does not mean they should stop functioning. It does mean that they should keep pride in check. We all have wild thoughts. It is of value to control the tongue and let no idle words come out.

It is not bad to be confident, have a great car and a great significant other. However, pride must be eliminated in to prevent disaster.

The best place to start is giving glory to God instead of self.

The next step is to think of ourselves with "sober judgment" remembering that only Christ is perfect—knowing that everyone has weaknesses they are susceptible to.

Finally, give thanks again and recognize that it is only because of Jesus's sacrifice that we have any standing on earth or heaven.

Ever-Changing:

A Super Hero Manual Book

Chapter 12: Down Days

When you don't want to lift a finger and the world is moving faster than you, just pray. Some days it's difficult to get inspired. Some days I just want to sleep. On these days, just about everyone meshes with me the wrong way.

It's a down day—a great way to develop empathy.

Can breakthrough happen on a "down day?" My friend, that would be a breakthrough!

"For we walk by faith, not by sight (2 Corinthians 5:7)."

It may feel difficult to pull breakthrough out of a "down day," "but with God all things are possible (Matthew 19:26)."

The Lord God will "never leave" me "nor forsake" me. I find my rest in the Lord Almighty. I need His comfort, His Voice in my life. I rest in Him and I am safe.

Even at this moment, I am no longer down. I go through fluctuations. But through it all, God is with me. When I feel idle, I need to ask, Lord what do you want me to do?

What's on your heart Creator?

Keep going. Keep running that race. Everyone has "down days."

<u>Ever-Changing:</u>

<u>A Super Hero Manual Book</u>

Chapter 13: Philosophical Sanity

Is a break from sanity a holiness divergence? I want to be real, but it seems enjoyable to play the game of relapse.

What is right? What is wrong? Is it in the eye of the Beholder? Are there absolutes?

Am I writing this book?

Does God exist?

Philosophy is what it wants to be—including a break from sanity.

Unraveling the details and rearranging them—as if we were gods. If we are, who holds the stars in the sky?

Humans are born with inherent fallibilities.

We have found a way to get to the Moon, but the Universe?

I think not.

Humans have a habit of declaring absolute knowledge about what they haven't experienced.

If it's on the History Channel, it must be true.

Explain to me why God isn't real, when He speaks to me every day.

Should I be committed to a hospital for hearing the Voice of Truth?

One day, that may be a reality. The consequences of a belief system may result in sending a Christ-follower to eternity to dwell with Him.

To some, that is more of a reward than a punishment.

The Bible says, "For God did not give us a spirit of fear, but of power, of love, and of a sound mind (2 Timothy 1:7)."

Perhaps, it is definite that veering from sanity deliberately is sin itself.

What if the purpose you are acting—is to play a part in stage production that builds awareness?

It seems that there is a place for deliberate breeches of sanity, but in the real world typically not.

How a person behaves is between him/her and God. This is the same God I talk to on a daily basis.

I just want to be real. I need to stop putting on a show. If I'm going to be a "fool," let it be for Christ. My Judge is the Lord!

<u>Ever-Changing:</u>

<u>A Super Hero Manual Book</u>

Chapter 14: In The Sun

Definition:

Spotlight, Focus, Star-Struck, Focal Point, In The Limelight

Key Verse:

"Humble yourselves in the sight of the Lord and He shall lift you up (James 4:10)."

Our focus needs to be on Christ. Christ was focused on glorifying the Father. We are to model after Him.

Christ set an example and lived a perfect life. He is God incarnate. No man/woman should put the focus on another man/woman or Super Hero for humankind is fallible.

Thank you Jesus for your patience with me. So often I focus on myself-- trying to be a Super Star for my own glory.

Not even Jesus tried to be the Super Star. He gave all glory unto God. A Super Star falls unless that Super Star is the Godhead.

Even though a member of the Godhead, Christ, was a Super Star, He took the nature of a servant and became obedient to death on a cross. (Philippians 2)

If a person takes a leadership role in this world, they should do it in humility. This is labeled "servant leadership." A servant leader concentrates on serving those he/she leads over and submitting to the leading of the Holy Spirit.

Question:
What do you think the Lord might be leading you to do today?

Ever-Changing:

A Super Hero Manual Book

Chapter 15: Neighbor's House

Key Verse: "Love your neighbor as yourself (Mark 12:31)."

You may be placed in a culture that is different from you. This is a gift from God. Differences make up diversity. Differences can be acclimated to. Differences should not be assumed to be evil on account of difference.

When at your neighbor's house, play by your neighbor's cultural rules—even if they are different from your own.

For instance, it is proper in many houses to take off your shoes.

Apostle Paul, faced cultural cues when he wrote a large part of the New Testament. His cultural standards applied to the Corinthian Church in that cultural time period.

We are to respect the cultural standards of different people's groups without assuming they are religious standards.

For instance, in Arabic countries, it seems to be the tradition to display religious texts on high places. The bathroom or floor is considered disrespectful.

We need to make an effort to "be all things to all people as to win some" for Christ.

Why lose an audience over traditional matters?

Respect the culture of others.

It is discourteous to negatively judge the mood of a Super Hero. As moods can fluctuate from moment to moment, encouragement works best.

Misery does not always love company.

In fact, the worst action you can take can be saying to a miserable creature: "You look depressed today."

Stay away from that label. On the same token, do not tell a jolly soul, "You seem manic."

Let a man enjoy his pleasing feeling. If he says something out of line, correct what he said—not the happy mood!

For many excuses exist to be non-functioning. I have written many chapters in a so-called altered state. If I was constantly waiting to be in an ideal mood—nothing would get done!

Give people grace. They serve God and do not bow down to you.

Let happy people be jolly. Let normal people praise God. Let sad people be encouraged.

Let everyone give thanks for being "alive and well."

Ever-Changing:

A Super Hero Manual Book

Chapter 17: Flesh

Word Association:

Being human, frail, of the world, sinful nature.

Is the flesh psychotic? It very well might be. For it brings death. It cannot please God.

In this culture, people use their illness(es) to explain their behaviors.

Yet, we are not of this world. We are to be set apart and live differently.

Can someone diagnosed Schizoaffective honor God?

"With God all things are possible (Mark 10:27)."

Yes, we are given a sound mind to claim. But are we to judge someone because they received a diagnosis from man—absolutely not!

Mister Energy Plus needs to determine to honor God whether up or down. He is proud of the uniqueness afforded to Him by God.

If he's not ashamed,
If he's obeying God,

Who are you to rain on his parade?

Thanks be to God.

"Let everything that has breath praise the Lord (Psalm 150:6)."

Ever-Changing:

A Super Hero Manual Book

Chapter 18: New Breakthrough

"His mercies begin afresh each morning. ... they are new every morning (Lamentations 3:23);" We must not forget, in the hour of New Breakthrough, that God is building the house. Everything we have is from Him. When we wake up in the morning, it's mercy. When we are forgiven each and every time, His mercy extends to us.

Sometimes I feel unworthy of that mercy, but feel I have to have good recovery time.

When I break God's policies, I should seek to have God fix the relationship ASAP. I want to have communication with God.

This is only possible with "mercies" that "are new every morning."

I am thankful that God is always faithful to me, unlike myself. His perfection and consistency holds me together.

Praise the Lord.

Ever-Changing:

A Super Hero Manual Book

Chapter 19: Blah...

When motivation is not there, what's the best action to take? People expect us to have the inspiration. God is in us after all.

In these situations, we have to dig deeper. We have to climb into the depths of our soul, where the Holy Spirit dwells.

It's time to get alone with Our Maker.

"But the Comforter, which is the Holy Ghost, whom the Father will send in my name. He will teach you all things and bring all things to your remembrance (John 14:26)."

God help us because really who else can? Some have fought the same fight before, but there is an hour where everyone else is busy or asleep.

Jesus experienced this moment in the Garden of Gethsemane. We are surrounded by such a great cloud of witnesses. We cannot give up the fight!

We must plough ahead when we do not feel like it and build our spiritual/emotional muscles.

"With my God I can scale any wall (Psalm 18:29)."

On my own, I rot on earth and in Hell.

I need Jesus to function, literally.

When, "I am weak, He is strong (Jesus Loves Me This I Know)."

Thank you Lord!

Ever-Changing:

A Super Hero Manual Book

Chapter 20: Impulse

My first thought is not always the best. Stopping to pray is wisdom. Carnality has a tendency to come out with impulse.

Super Heroes veer on the side of impulsive tendencies when their diagnoses fall in the manic spectrum.

I would venture to hypothesize, having had swings of depression, any mental condition polar of normal can bring impulsive tendencies.

The best way to cope is with love. Surround yourself in the love of God and with people who love God. Go to God first, for people can let you down. God will, "never leave" us "nor forsake" us.

Serving God is real and is the best default decision. Consider your words and daily actions carefully. People are watching closely.

Some are sizing up whether they believe Christianity is real.
Some are taking us to be hypocritical.

Some are seeing the Light of God in us.

Do not be guilt-ridden over the past impulsive mistakes. They can be forgiven and then washed away as white as snow. No memory is left of them—in God's mind. Do not be held down by others' bitterness. Move on and be blessed.

Chapter 21: Smorgasbord

Heaven is not the only place that "my soul shall be delighted as with the richest of foods." Life on earth is a blessing for those who sit at God's table.

"You prepare a table in the presence of my enemies. You anoint my head with oil (Psalm 23:5)."

The blessed anointing is strong true believers who know the Spirit. They walk forward and blessings flow. "For we walk by faith, not by sight (2 Corinthians 5:7)."

It is a smorgasbord of spiritual food.

"For the kingdom of God is not a matter of eating and drinking, but of righteousness, peace and joy in the Holy Spirit (Romans 14:7)."

We are to be filled in such a way that does not end in a tummy ache. Instead, we are supposed to overfill like a fresh spring—sharing the precipitation of God's love with everyone.

"You prepare a table for me in the presence of my enemies. You anoint my head with oil. My cup overflows (Psalm 23:5,6)."

This overflowing love flows with a presence that knows **God is real.**

This is the blessing for true believers.

Getting filled with the Holy Ghost is not a magic occurrence but rather the reality of a satisfied soul that must share because he/she is bursting at the seams with joy.

Enter into the joy of the Lord. Open your Bible and ask God how.

"All things are possible with God (Mark 10:27)."

"Surely goodness and mercy shall follow me all the days of my life and I shall dwell in the house of the Lord forever (Psalm 23:6)."

Ever-Changing:

A Super Hero Manual Book

Chapter 22: Help

After the shock is over, no one wants to be "The Boy Who Cried Wolf."

There are ramifications to sounding the alarm. Consequences exist in this life for playing the attention-getter.

Yet, what if these emergencies are real and constant? What if we lived in a body in torment?

Would people cease to care about us? Would we become frustrated to the point of sounding the alarm?

Suffering is real and we must not be insensitive to those in chronic pain. I know of a young man who goes to the hospital frequently for different reasons.

His faith journey must be slightly different than mine and I do not know how to encourage him in his frustrating pain. What should I say? What should I do?

I will just be there for him.

A person suffering from chronic emergencies appreciates someone being there with him/her.

It can be lonely to suffer in isolation. I have family. I cannot imagine if I did not.

Perhaps, we are this person's family.

Be sensitive to those who suffer from chronic pain. Listen as best you can.

You may be entertaining an angel unaware.

Ever-Changing:

A Super Hero Manual Book

Chapter 23: Leisure

What a person does for leisure pertains to what he/she values.

Are we just "passing the time" or are we intentional about how we spend our "free time?"

Some are very busy, yet can pencil others in. Some have constant free time and still do not make time for others.

It seems there is always time for our priorities.

What are our priorities and do we consciously implement them into all aspects of life?

It is a mistake to fixate on priorities we cannot control. However, if we do not keep priorities in mind on some level, we may lose sight of them.

Obituaries are not what many people want to think about from day to day. Yet, legacy does become a priority when time grows short.

What is important at the beginning typically changes by the end of one's life.

The rare people do not live last minute fix-it-up lives, rather consistent lives over time.

Daily they build into their legacy piggy-bank, treasures in Heaven.

I think of one of them. He just passed away into Glory Land.

His name is Charles Leverich. He had poems to share and let his generosity speak through his finances to the audience of one—God.

I imagine that this man's spare time, his leisure, was investing in others.

He will never be forgotten.

I want what I do to make a lasting impression on God' face. Right now, I am not selfless enough.

I let my mood be effected by circumstances from time to time. Still I know Jesus is Lord and I want to live for Him!

Super Heroes can be marginalized, but God knows their true legacy.

He is the final audience. As Paul said, "To live is Christ; to die is gain (Philippians 1:21)."

Let us live and prioritize our lives with eternal perspective.

Ever-Changing:

A Super Hero Manual Book

Chapter 24: Love

If you read 1 John quickly, you may summarize that to continue sinning is not to know God.

Looking, closely, there is a provision made for repentance.

1 John 1:9 "If we confess our sins, He is faithful and just to forgive our sins and to cleanse us from all unrighteousness."

Love is what it's all about. Love for God and fellow man is the summary of the Scripture – especially love for enemies.

It is time to take a stand for righteousness and care for those in need.

It is time to be set apart and have that saltiness that makes Christians different—being uniquely salty.

People are hurting and when we are in sin, our spirits are hurting.

Love is what's needed to change the world—not the condemnation of the devil.

Shall we hold back the truth because it offends?

God forbid. Walk the right path and testify to the goodness of God!

If we as believers do not speak up, who will bring the good news? "Beautiful are the feet of them which bring good news (Romans 10:15)!"

Ever-Changing:

A Super Hero Manual Book

Chapter 25: Take Me Home

There will be a day, when all pain is gone. We will have new bodies. "But as it is written, Eye hath not seen, nor ear heard, neither have entered into the heart of man, the things which God hath prepared for them that love him (1 Corinthians 2:9)." I've never seen Heaven, but it will be better than anything I could ever imagine. Surely, it will be deep Communion with the Everlasting God.

No more curses. No more pain. No more light needed; for the glory of the Lord will shine. One focus, One God, One Accord. We will come together to praise the Lord.

It will be our passion to do this as it should be now. Let's "run in such a way as to get the prize (1 Corinthians 9:24)." Let's put Christ first in this life and the lay down our crowns in the next.

For God is worthy of all adoration.

Ever-Changing:

A Super Hero Manual Book

Chapter 26: Encouragement

There are moments when Super Heroes fall on the floor, down for the count, ready to tap out.

It is at these moments, "…We walk by faith, not by sight (2 Corinthians 5:7)." God is real and He will come through for His children in unexpected ways.

Where does my hope from when everyone has fled the scene? God is my hope and "God works in mysterious ways."

Mysterious: The despised people looked down upon can be there for you in your time of need.

"But God chose the foolish things of the world to shame the wise (1 Corinthians 1:27);"

Today, a street minister cared about me when I left the building where ministry was taking place.

I did not know she and her team cared so much. They prayed over me immediately. They stopped the order of the meeting for me—one soul.

This is how God's heart operates.

There is more joy in Heaven when one sinner repents than over a fold of 100 righteous.

You can lightly sprinkle a congregation of a hundred or can drench one desperate parched soul on the brink of disaster.

Thank you Jesus for sending a seemingly invisible ministry to reach the invisible.

Use their work to change the world—one city at a time.

Conclusion:

Encouragement becomes epic when it considers every last soul.

Ever-Changing:

A Super Hero Manual Book

Chapter 27: Sticking With It

The Bible says, "We will reap a harvest if we don't give up (Galatians 6:9)." Investing in people is a huge, meaningful, endeavor.

When we pour into lives, we pour into souls. We must have substance ourselves, something to give, but every deposit counts.

Do not give up on people. See hope in every life, every opportunity. Stand your ground for the Lord as a good soldier. Love always. Never quit loving.

Never give up on a person this side of Heaven. The Lord knows the heart. We are meant to see hope.

"For I know the plans I have for you," declares the LORD, "plans to prosper you and not to harm you, plans to give you hope and a future (Jeremiah 29:11)." Never let up. If you give up on a person or a person's vision, you may injure that person's motivation.

See the hope in every soul and give your best to investing in others.

It will reap eternal dividends.

Morale:

Take eyes off self and love others to the end as Christ loved and gave Himself for us.

Chapter 28: Deletion

Defined:

Removal, Microsoft Trash, To Take Away, Eliminate.

No more. No More. Many times, it seems, life has friends that shouldn't be around. Full-throttle, for whatever reason, the Super Hero may believe he/she needs to go on a deleting spree.

Overkill, is overkill. Hopefully, no bridges have been burned.

When a Super Hero does not know what to do, he/she might hit the delete button. Bye-Bye career, Bye-Bye Church and the friends that goes with it!

The secret to happiness is not always CTRL-ALT-DELETE. Sometimes there is a backdoor.

However, everyone needs a vacation once in awhile. Basically, no one has it all together all the time. Give Super Heroes a little breathing room so we can breathe. You will be thankful you did.

Ever-Changing:

A Super Hero Manual Book

Chapter 29: Reality

I want to write something incredible, weighty, substantial, and real.

My reality is Jesus Christ. I do not claim to understand every perplexity, preponderance, or supposed contradiction.

All I claim is that He is in me and for me. All I can testify is that He has improved my life and the life of others.

Does the History Channel dispute God? Not anymore than the original Adversary, challenging liar did when he put himself out of paradise.

Dynasties will rise and dynasties will fall. The truth of God remains applicable to my life.

I may not always apply it. I may not always live by it, but I walk by the faith that reveals itself with time.

We all need a Comforter, a God who communicates with us.

We may not always hear clearly, but the music is playing.

"For we walk by faith not by sight (2 Corinthians 5:7)."

Ever-Changing:

A Super Hero Manual Book

Chapter 30: Where (Many) Super Heroes Worship

When there is no place to go, this is where people go. City Outreach, aka Bozzo's is a place of mercy, for many of Lansing's broken on Sunday Morning.

There is food, love, mercy, rough edges meeting rough edges. I think of Jesus reaching the 12 disciples with raw love, boldness.

Not everyone is smiling, in fact many are screaming inside. Some haven't had a good night sleep in the changing Michigan weather in months.

This is the place where love shines down through food, a rebuke, an effortful smile.

Jesus said, "The King will reply, 'Truly I tell you, whatever you did for one of the least of these brothers and sisters of mine, you did for me (Matthew 25:40)." This is Lansing's hotspot of "faith, hope, and love."

Ever-Changing:

A Super Hero Manual Book

Chapter 31: Waiting

Breakthrough does not happen overnight always. Breakthrough usually takes a tremendous amount of mental effort called faith.

Hold it together. Do not give up. Push forward by faith.

With man it may be impossible. "But with God all things are possible (Matthew 19:26)."

Never let up on living. Never let up on waiting for God's promises to come to pass. You may be waiting for provision, a career, the right spouse to come into your life.

In your time of waiting, obey God, serve God, be thankful! Read the Bible and stand on it.

"Faith is the substance of things hoped for, the evidence of things unseen (Hebrews 11:1)." Take the time to not just wait for your own miracle, but be the God-send miracle in another's life!

Love "always hopes, trusts, perseveres (1 Corinthians 13:7)." Persevere in being a good, giving, loving soldier and know that your blessing is coming.

"Delight thyself also in the LORD;
and he shall give thee the desires of thine heart (Psalm 37:4)."

What do you desire most?

What is important to you?

When we bless others while waiting, our world can turn right side up!

Live your dreams.

If you aren't paid, see your dreams come to pass pro bono.

Watch God take care of you! His love is unending.

Serving the broken is serving Him.

Theme:

Do the work of the Lord as you wait to see your dreams come to pass by faith.

<u>Ever-Changing:</u>

<u>A Super Hero Manual Book</u>

Chapter 32: Conclusion

Life is an ever-changing world. Today is not the same as yesterday. "Tomorrow is not promised." The present is not to be worried about and can change.

You have read these pages about the life of a Super Hero. Where the saga begins is of little importance compared to the journey and destination.

Share the journey. Run the race. Do not give up.

Thanks,

Daniel K. Arnold

Book III

Black Bird Ops:

A Super Hero Manual Book

by

Daniel K. Arnold

Black Bird Ops:

A Super Hero Manual Book

Chapter 1

This may be a new tale for you. Have you ever met someone really out of it?

Have you ever met a person going on an adventure in his/her own head?

Meet the realm of Black Bird Ops—introduced in the small companion book, Everchanging. He's real, yet he's a façade. He's this Super Hero's favorite delusion.

And he's going "undercover." Some call him a night owl. Typically, he won't wear sunglasses unless the mission calls for it.

He believes he's an American hero, but at times it's a façade to boost his hurting self-esteem.

Black Bird Ops absorbs any information leading him to sound more trendy and real. He dreams of being a special agent and wonder if he's already been recruited.

He is deluded in this persona and partially under the confusion of satan.

Black Bird Ops, the character of schizoaffective, originated from 'normalcy' and evolved to Mister Energy Plus. Finally, after enough stress Black Bird Ops became my coping mechanism.

As I talked about semi-sensitive governmental terminology, I began to relive the seemingly covert world in my sleep.

Chapter 2

There is no logical explanation for the origins of this Super Hero gone Black Bird Ops! I can only attempt to piece together Schizoaffective for the world through a diagnosis that is Bipolar with paranoid Schizophrenic features.

During the day, this persona does not usually come out.

At night, it feels natural for this character to want to be productive as it is sleepless and lonely.

Help me oh Lord to overcome Black Bird Ops. I need help!

Studies have shown the insomnia side of Abilify and that plays a part in the adventure.

Abilify is a part of Black Bird Ops's arsenal without choice. Because Abilify is now injected into the Super Hero, the description of Abilify implants in his legs seems appropriate.

Not everyone who is Schizoaffective takes Abilify, therefore Black Bird Ops's description in this book may seem somewhat unique and that leaves the character ever eager to reach out to others.

Black Bird Ops is fascinated by similar characters like Deep Skull but at the same time they have a tendency to scare him.

Delusions are not cool no matter how glamorous they seem.

Black Bird Ops you need to leave in the name of Jesus!

Chapter 3

I live my days with a semblance of sanity. Few know of my secret night life except other cronies. It's a "dog eat dog eat dog world out there."

Who can you trust under the guise of the night?

It's nighttime and this night is atypical.

I did not wake up every hour on the hour with fearful night terror hallucinations.

Instead, I had a normal dream and woke up after 2am thankful for a semblance of sanity.

Thank you Jesus.

No bugs, mice, poop delusions of things in my pants.

Nope, just peace.

Thank you Jesus. He told me I would get more sleep. I am thankful now for therapy because I badly need it.

I am on a blood-work fast for twelve hours now and I want me some comfort food!

I want some soda in the fridge. I want some sort of "creature comfort."

Oh, it is life. I will wait for correct labs because I need to get better.

Black Bird Ops:

A Super Hero Manual Book

Chapter 4

I've tested the effects of cutting out the medication Abilify many times.

I insist on going against the medical consensus.

As Mister Energy Plus I can be a real rebel and as Black Bird Ops I can get real desperate. Together, they make a one-of-a-kind shifting persona.

Black Bird Ops you have to leave, but I am tempted to keep a little Mister Energy Plus buzz in my steps.

Normal doesn't always seem that appealing.

"Welcome to the Super Hero life of relying on God and eachother."

Black Bird Ops:

A Super Hero Manual Book

Chapter 5

I have the urge to write, but my body is fatigued. It is 5:40am and I am riding on the bus around Lansing, Michigan, USA.

Yawn.. "Good Morning America." Slowly getting up.

Praise the Lord. I am thankful for a hero like Ricky who reminded me to follow the Holy Spirit.

This ride is bumpy and I don't have a lot on my mind. Yet, I am thankful for my family, friends, God and readership.

God Bless you all!

God Bless the suffering right now. God Bless those out on the streets with sleepless nights. God Bless the beggars and those in pain.

God Bless the needy and abused over and over again. Rescue them from "harm's way" and show them your love oh God.

Have mercy on the brokenhearted and the ones that cannot defend themselves. Reach out to the meek and lowly. Grant them peace, forevermore.

You see I just had a little tiny bitter taste. I have not suffered again and again like others.

And my eternity is glory land if I should so continue in God's kindness.

Lord, have mercy on the suffering. Lord, restore what was lost.

Help us all to forgive in the name of Jesus, Amen.

Let us pray as Jesus demonstrated on the cross at Calvary: "Lord forgive them for they know not what they do."

<u>Black Bird Ops:</u>

A Super Hero Manual Book

Chapter 6

Have you ever been severely wronged and the incident was swept under the rug?

We must learn to forgive yet take action when necessary.

Justice is tricky business. For we are expected to act justly despite what anyone else does. There is only room to keep one's own integrity and remember:

"Vengeance is mine saieth the Lord."

We cannot take matters into our own hands, but we can take a course of action to protect ourselves.

In my situation, I was a whistleblower. I filled boxes with complaints that were ignored in their abundance.

I was a real button-pusher. Why? Because I'm a natural written creative communicator. I like to see my thoughts on paper and get the message out.

If I have input, I am determined to get results.

What am I to do when I really need justice? I assumed tell everyone in authority until someone reacts.

Wrong.

The proper answer is logical. Go through the chain of commands.

Pray to God and go to the most immediate person in authority.

After praying, contact the Recipient Rights Office most proximate to the location of the rights violation.

Next, do not give up on appeals.

Always forgive!

Never stop learning and teaching others from what you learn from your difficult experiences.

Put everything in God's hands and move on.

Do not let an incident hold you back back from your future. Finally, do not withhold justice when others are being harmed.

Forgiveness is difficult. Sometimes justice must be left in the hands of God.

Black Bird Ops:

A Super Hero Manual Book

Chapter 7

Door (A) is closed.

Door (B) is opening.

There is hope for you and for me. We are blessed. When Option #1 is no longer an option, do not sweat it!

God may be opening a door to your destiny that "no man can shut!"

I believed I was meant to be a school teacher. I did not know when I failed teacher internship that there were other options left.

It seemed like the end of the line, but God had other plans.

"Plans to prosper me and not to harm me, plans to give me a hope and a future (Bible)."

Now I write books and edit newsletters. God is on the move and He'll use you if you'll let Him. Do not let go of Plan (B) when and if Plan (A) fails. Move down the line until you find the right one.

It took multiple tries for Einstein to find the right light bulb configuration. The same goes true for life at times

Black Bird Ops:

A Super Hero Manual Book

Chapter 8

Q: When is enough, enough?

A: The day I die.

I will not be satisfied unless I productively make something of myself day after day.

If you've written a good poem, do not stop there. Write more the next day. Be consistent. "Finish what you start."

Create a legacy.

Super Heroes exist in part to inspire others. Do some good works. Make a difference for Jesus. Be real in this lifetime.

Discipleship is a great way to do this. One by one, student by student. Investment instead of scattershot.

Breakthrough lesson learned. Change can happen today by the power of God.

Be an inspiration to someone else a few steps behind you on the journey.

Do not be afraid to reach out to motivated individuals older, younger, or the same age as you.

Imagine having other Super Heroes tutored by you accompanied by their own unique giftings.

Perhaps, they have a thing or two to teach you too! This is inspired by God. "Bear one another's burdens."

Love at all times. Never give up on life. We are blessed!

Black Bird Ops:

A Super Hero Manual Book

Chapter 9

Super Heroes need extra space to compensate for their, shall we say, idiosyncrasies. Not everyone shares the same place. This is true of Black Bird Ops.

A person of his/her inkling enjoys his own space while simultaneously being codependent.

Go figure.

This means he wants freedom, but the ability to use others' space when convenient.

Imagine the anger of having your place trashed for the enjoyment of the co-dependent Super Hero.

Every character is unique, especially among Super Heroes, because God made no two the same.

How do we cope with this monstrocity— communication, forgiveness and love?

They go a long way in building and maintaining relationships.

It is not proper to abruptly write people off— unless they try to burn down the house or spur on a police call.

Even there, there is a place for letting go, starting over, and saying, "I will be one of this guy or gal's few friends," like Jesus.

"Whatsoever you do unto the least of these brethren, you do unto me."

Be Jesus to the spiritually blind. Let your life give them eyes to see.

Chapter 10

Squeezing turnips. Asking for something when nothing is there. Not being realistic. "Kicking him now that he's down."

Sometimes Super Heroes are too depleted to move a muscle.

Sometimes Super Heroes fake this because they choose to.

Reality hurts, but at times pain is good. Pain can be a motivator. Pain as punishment can turn a sinner from his/her wicked ways.

Do not be afraid to inflict a little pain, but be mindful of the weakened sickness of the Super Hero.

A man who is depressed may not have the strength to move and a depleted angry OCD person may be extremely bothered finding deposits not his own in his place of dwelling.

When Ice Man meets Mister Energy Plus in the middle of the night (Black Bird Ops) for confrontation, look out!

Both now have little patience. Ice Man has energy because of his anger.

Black Bird Ops is in emergency crash mode talking like a private eye detective.

Fireworks may ensue and it might be a good time to wait until morning for the storm to clear.

Otherwise, the exchange may become unforgettable!

In short, make big allowances for Super Heroes as you have not walked in their enormous or teeny shoes.

Black Bird Ops:

A Super Hero Manual Book

Chapter 11

Morning America. I am sleepy. I chose to wake up early. I mean to stay awake. Life is full of decisions moment by moment that add up.

This is true of the typical Super Hero diet. Some grab excessive caffeine like Mister Energy Plus. Others grab beer after beer to try to get some cheer (or simply go to sleep).

And it seems to work for the moment. As blocks of dependency are built upon dependency, an addictive tendency seems to commence in many Super Heroes.

Call it self-medicating, but much of the Super Hero populations seems irresponsible in substance intake to cope with the pain they are facing.

What seems like idiosyncrasies actually shortens life. It's reality. Where's the solution?

Turn from your sin seems to be the too simple answer for the suffering Super Hero.

A little sensitivity, compassion and peer support goes a long way.

Sometimes you have to have been there to have the empathy to understand.

Yet, everyone has the capacity to love, listen, and extend forgiveness.

And point out those epic qualities that make Super Heroes super!

Chapter 12

I am blessed, but sometimes I am ashamed. Not everyone believes in my receiving lifestyle. I am told SSI will not last. I am told to get a job and stop faking it.

Let me tell you, four books and twenty-five pages of newsletters later, I am not here to play around.

I have a message and a destiny.

I am purposeful and I am not giving up. I have suffered burn out, but my heart is very much alive.

I desire to see breakthrough in my life and yours.

I t is not the place of a non-physician to judge whether someone is able to work. This is between a person and his/her doctor.

Writing is my job. It is no more dignified than any other work and no less despite having no paycheck to show for it.

I'm thankful for God's provision and aim to give back to society through writing.

Chapter 13

They say, "There is no free lunch," but in Lansing God provides. He's there for people when they are not there for themselves.

Salvation Army, Volunteers of America, the nicknamed "Chocolate Milk Church" to name a few.

God provides out of the service and pockets of others. We should be grateful as a society for what we are provided and not ashamed or judging.

"The rain falls on the good and bad alike."

Do not give up on reaching out no matter what position you are in in society. The job needs to get done regardless.

"Love at all times." "If at all possible, be at peace with everyone."

Reach the unreachable with simple orchestrated or unorchestrated acts of kindness.

Love with sincerity for our attitudes can be read. Motive shines out of the heart attitude.

Be unique. Love your enemies. Do good to them that persecute you. Never let up. Show mercy like Jesus.

When you serve, your breakthrough is just around the corner.

Black Bird Ops:

A Super Hero Manual Book

Chapter 14

Dreams do not come true overnight—necessarily. Have faith in God to move mountains in your time of need.

While you tarry, give thanks to God for everything. "God works out all things to the good of those that love God and are called according to His purpose."

Be faithful. Breakthrough comes at an unknown timing. When seeking breakthroughs it is important to seek out eternal treasure rather than simply material success.

We are told in the Bible that "We will reap a harvest if we don't give up."

This harvest can be described as legacy. Some people do not see the difference they've made until after-life. Eternal reward is great reward.

I go on to say vision must be carried out if it is of the Lord. All the powers in Hell cannot prevail against it. Success will happen, though not always seen with the naked eye.

"I can do all things through Christ who strengthens me."

This is a vision for him/her who believes. Do not let go of it. We all need to live as we are leaving a legacy.

People are famished in many different ways. They need our inspiration that comes from God.

Be a light as He is a light.

Watch the darkness flee.

Wahooo!

Be led by the Spirit and make a difference in your sphere of influence.

If you are a painter, paint.
If you are a talker, talk the truth.

If you smile and encourage, don't give up when the going gets tough!

People are listening, reading, talking, thinking. Be an inspiration.

Black Bird Ops:

A Super Hero Manual Book

Chapter 15

Super Heroes are human. They sin on purpose. It is no accident. They commit willful sin with the knowledge of the truth-- living like they do not know better.

Sowing to the flesh is death and Super Heroes are without excuse.

Now is the time to pick up our feet again. The hour of repentance is here!

"Seek Him while He may be found. Call on Him while He is near."

Now is the time to turn our hearts back to God—to begin living the abundant life. For sin does not satisfy but for a moment.

And, then an empty condemning feeling is all that is left.

Let us leave this pattern of transgression and turn to the Lord. Let us learn to live 100% for God and God alone.

The past is the past. Be free. Repent and return to Jesus. Let us live a new life—a free life a happy life.

"Blessed is he who does not walk in the counsel of the ungodly, nor standeth in the way of sinners, nor sit in the seat of scoffers (Psalm 1:1)."

It is time to clear the runway for Jesus. Let us walk a straight path and associate with men and women who follow Him. Let us take the time to rest and the time to walk.

Let us serve wholeheartedly.

And zoom to the horizon as Super Heroes.

Black Bird Ops:

A Super Hero Manual Book

Chapter 16

If you cannot play the music, let someone gifted take the lead in that department.

Do not be a showboat; be a humble inspiration.

Look to Jesus first and humble people second. Find inspiration and know that people are imperfect.

People let us down, but God will never let us down.

"God demonstrates His love for us in this, while we were yet sinners, Christ died for us."

We can find people nonetheless who are great examples, great inspirers, great livers of the faith.

"Without faith it is impossible to please Him."

I am waiting on the Lord for a miracle-- change in my life.

Yet I must take action. I must live out by faith and take a step of faith.

"With God all things are possible."

Black Bird Ops:

A Super Hero Manual Book

Chapter 17

We have been entrusted with some. Let us be faithful with some. For God gives the increase.

God can and will make a good mountain out of a good molehill.

So "run the race as to get the prize."

Your breakthrough is on its way. What do we live for?

Our answer should be to love God and others. Everything else falls into place.

"Seek first the Kingdom of God and His righteousness and all these things shall be added unto you."

God brings the increase when we seek Him first.

SideNote: Right now my head is sweating, my head is pounding and I'm concerned about manic symptoms.

Yet I know, God is in control and bringing my dream to pass as we speak.

Today, I am more motivated than yesterday. I am dreaming for my future. I see God at the center of it.

"For I know the plans I have for you, plans to prosper you and not to harm you, plans to give you hope and a future."

God cares about my future and can use "bad news" for His purpose.

With God's impact upon even dire circumstances, tragedies can actually turn into breakthrough through God's broken people—Super Heroes.

You may not realize it, but you are a Super Hero. Even if you are diagnosed mentally ill and looked down upon by society, you matter.

You are crucial. You are needed for society to function. God makes all the difference in marginalized lives and seemingly ideal lives.

God wants us to continue in His kindness, serve Him and be faithful.

Faithfulness reaps a harvest if we do not give up.

Your moment of breakthrough is now. A changed mind is a changed life by the power of God.

Saul changed his mind and became Paul. Abram changed his mind and became Abraham.

These new people were appointed new identities by God—applying their past to change the world.

The past is over, but its applications are not forgotten. Your calling begins now, but was created by God long before. Get excited!

Black Bird Ops:

A Super Hero Manual Book

Chapter 18

What do we look for in change? Do we elicit it in others or go about it in our own lives first?

We need to look at our own selves with a microscope before studying others flaws.

Let the little things pass to make room for new things.

It seems that I cannot write now, but God knows what He is doing.

He created me. He created you for a purpose.

It is time to move forward. Praise the Lord. We can do this with each other and with God!

"I waited for the Lord on high and He heard my cry. He pulled me out of the miry and set me feet upon a rock."

I know breakthrough is here and will continue to come. We are victors!

Book IV

All Scripture used is taken from the New

International Version and The King James Version

of the Bible.

2nd Edition

Copyright Daniel Keith Arnold 2016,

Lansing Riverfront Press

Dedicated to the Passionate Believers I once

opposed and to Jesus Christ who paid the ultimate

price for truth.

OBEY GOD.

By

DANIEL K. ARNOLD

Obey God.

By Daniel K. Arnold

Testimony

I was distant. I did not know the requirements of my God and was wise in my own eyes. When I met the initial preachers, they seemed a turn-off, shouting that true repentance and change was necessary.

I created a piece of writing and made 150 copies to oppose them. One day, behind them God sent in reinforcements. A marine veteran shared his testimony and kindly invited me to Bible Study. He seemed noble and nice enough. When I went to the Bible Study I was horrified to hear the same message again. I stopped up my ears.

In my time of need, the door opened and I returned. One person planted a seed. One watered it, "but God made it grow."

You never know the complete results of your faithfulness to God! I told the man if he could possibly persuade me to the truth about repentance, I would tell the world.

In 2009, I wrote a long Facebook post about this message. In 2014, I converted it into the book, The Super Hero Manual II: Facilitating a Hideout Bible Study. In 2016, I finalized the book and as I read my words to edit, the Scripture had an effect on my heart again.

The Word does not return void. God's Word is living and active, real. My heart changed. Change can happen to anyone with "ears to hear." If you agree, pass this book on to your neighbor. Plant a seed. Let God make it grow

Obey God.

By Daniel K. Arnold

Chapter 1

"There is a way that seemeth right unto a man, but the end thereof *are* the ways of death (Proverbs 16:25, KJV)."

Popular Culture, Social Media, Life's Happenings. What seems right frequently is not right. Moral Truth is unchanging. There are absolutes. Whether someone calls himself/herself "heroic" or "ordinary," there exists an internal need to submit to a Higher Power.

Order involves submission. Order involves acknowledging that we are not God. In an age of moral relativism, where people redefine their own realities, who is there to turn to but God and His Holy Word?

The inspired Word of God can and will change lives.

In this new part of the year, written in January, almost everyone is aiming for a New Year's Resolution. People rarely shoot for the moon anymore though because they do not believe they can reach it. They have given up!

People have "tried faith" and it "didn't work."

The Bible says, "Ye lust, and have not: ye kill, and desire to have, and cannot obtain: ye fight and war, yet ye have not, because ye ask not. Ye ask, and receive not, because ye ask amiss, that ye may spend it in your pleasures (James 4:2-3, KJV)."

Rather than shoot for your own moon this year, point, aim, and shoot for what God asks you to aim for. Point to the will of God. Aim through His Word as you seek Him in prayer and shoot for the moon by faith! God will help you bring His will for your life to pass. We must remain in the Vine of Christ.

"I am the vine, ye *are* the branches: He that abideth in me, and I in him, the same bringeth forth much fruit: for without me ye can do nothing (John 15:5, KJV)."

What does God require of us? There is a song
from the Bible that explains:

"He has shown thee.

He has shown thee O Man,

What is good and what the Lord requires of thee.

But to do justly,

But to do justly,

And to love mercy,
And to walk humbly with thy God."

Webster's New Universal Dictionary

"Just" a. is defined as 1. Upright, honest, having
principles of rectitude, righteous, as a just man.

Adv. Exactly, precisely

We should not live life by our own haphazard rules and morals. We need a Moral Code—the Bible— to live by. Our personal skewed definition of obedience misses the mark.

"For the wages of sin is death, but the gift of God is eternal life in Christ Jesus Our Lord (Romans 6:23)."

For "while we were yet sinners Christ died for us (Romans 5:8)." Now that we are restored to life, we must "continue in His kindness (Romans 11:22)."

We run the race with endurance.

Do you agree?

Or do you believe living for God is impossible?

Can we pick and choose how we are going to obey God's moral law?

This would be a conundrum; for there is forgiveness, but not license to sin.

"If we confess our sins, He is faithful and just to forgiveth our sins and to cleanse us from all unrighteousness (1 John 1:9)."

Who would take a bath and then throw select filth back on their body?

People are cleansed to be cleansed and to be as seen as blameless before Christ. Repenting is turning 180 degrees from our sin.

In the Book of Psalms, the Bible says, "As far as the east is from the west, so far has he removed our transgressions from us (Psalm 103:12, NIV)."

Why would we return to our sins if they only harm us?

"Whosoever committeth sin transgresseth also the law: for sin is the transgression of the law (1 John 3:4, KJV)."

The Holy Spirit convicts us of sin found in God's Moral Law the Bible.

"But the Comforter, which is the Holy Ghost, whom the Father will send in my name, he shall teach you all things, and bring all things to your remembrance, whatsoever I have said unto you (John 14:26, KJV)."

<u>Obey God.</u>

Chapter 2

The Doctrine of Repentance

I grew up believing the popular consensus about sin. I was raised in church. I believed if I sincerely prayed a prayer of salvation, I would be Heaven bound, no questions asked.

When I was told otherwise, by some unpopular people, I at first all-out rebelled. I even spread literature against their message! Yet, over time, when I was thirsty for it, I was shown the truth at a Bible Study. I decided I would never come back when I heard what was being spoken, but God brought me back!

Over time, I would transition to believe the message I once abhorred.

I learned from this study, that God expects my best sacrifice, my best heart. I never realized it before.

On this adventure I went, breathing in and out the truths of Scripture until there was absorption.

Prepare to be shocked and prepare to let God speak to you as He did me:

But the question is, "Do I truly love them if I don't tell the complete truth?"

Am I worried that I may be rejected if I speak an unpopular message?

"Who the Son sets free is free indeed."

What does that mean to you?

Does it just mean you are free from worrying about your eternal destination? Is that all it means?

That one day you confess all your sins and turn to Jesus and the next day you are doing drugs?

People have various explanations for this...

[Opening]

1. Well, you can't judge them because the Bible says, "Do not judge or you to will be judged (Matthew 7:1)."

Look further...

1 Corinthians 5:12-13 (NIV)

"What business is it of mine to judge those outside the church? Are you not to judge those inside? God will judge those outside. "Expel the wicked man from among you."

It is quite obvious that if God tell us in the New Testament to expel someone from the Church who calls themselves a Christian yet is walking in sin that if they aren't even welcome in a church on this imperfect earth, that they potentially might not be welcome in a perfect world. Besides, they are considered "wicked" by God.

Ephesians 5:3-5 (NIV)

"But among you there must not be even a hint of sexual immorality, or of any kind of impurity, or of greed, because these are improper for God's holy people. Nor should there be obscenity, foolish talk or coarse joking, which are out of place, but rather thanksgiving. For of this you can be sure: No immoral, impure or greedy person—such a man is an idolater—has any inheritance in the kingdom of Christ and of God."

So I ask you, what is the definition of an immoral person? What is the definition of a greedy person? And why is that person an idolater?

Some may reason that the definition of an immoral person is based on how they believe Christ views them, regardless of their actions.

1 John 1:5-6 (NIV)

"This is the message we have heard from him and declare to you: God is light; in him there is no darkness at all. If we claim to have fellowship with him yet walk in the darkness, we lie and do not live by the truth.

Most people know that to walk in darkness is to commit any sin at all.

And here is where further human reasoning comes into play....

Let's go LOGICAL here for a second:

IF God is against divorce and Christ is married to us,

THEN, it's all good!

For better or for worse, right?

There was an exception:

Matthew 5:31-32 (NIV)

"It has been said, 'Anyone who divorces his wife must give her a certificate of divorce.'I tell you that anyone who divorces his wife, except for marital unfaithfulness, causes her to become an adulteress, and anyone who marries the divorced woman commits adultery."

In the Old Testament, God DIVORCED his people for being an "adulterous nation."

"I gave faithless Israel her certificate of divorce and sent her away because of all her adulteries. Yet I saw that her unfaithful sister Judah had no fear; she also went out and committed adultery (Jeremiah 3:8, NIV)."

Adultery against God in this way was to have a "lover" in addition to God-- aka idolatry.

As we read in the New Testament:

"For of this you can be sure: No immoral, impure or greedy person—such a man is an idolater—has any inheritance in the kingdom of Christ and of God (Ephesians 5:5, NIV)."

The Issue of Sacrifice

It is common knowledge that God expected His children to walk uprightly in the Old Testament.

But of course, everyone sinned from time to time.

If they ever sinned, they had to sacrifice a perfect lamb and repent.

Then, their sin would, as much as possible, be overlooked by God.

New Testament Sacrifice

Now, that Jesus has died on the cross and rose again, He is the perfect sacrifice that allows us to be one with the Father. However, we must still confess our sins whenever we commit them.

"If we claim to be without sin, we deceive ourselves and the truth is not in us. If we confess our sins, he is faithful and just and will forgive us our sins and purify us from all unrighteousness (1 John 1:8-9, NIV)."

We sing songs that God never changes, but do we really believe it?

Do we somehow believe that God expected His children to walk in righteousness in the Old Testament and now we are free through Jesus to live like the devil?

Remain in me, and I will remain in you. No branch can bear fruit by itself; it must remain in the vine. Neither can you bear fruit unless you remain in me. "I am the vine; you are the branches. If a man remains in me and I in him, he will bear much fruit; apart from me you can do nothing. If anyone does not remain in me, he is like a branch that is thrown away and withers; such branches are picked up, thrown into the fire and burned (John 15:4-6, NIV)."

How do we know we are remaining in Him?

Is it when the pastor tells us not to worry and assures us of our salvation?

"For God is not the author of confusion, but of peace, as in all churches of the saints (1 Corinthians 14:33, KJV)."

We don't need a pastor to do this. We need God. He is our final judge.

"But the righteousness that is by faith says: "Do not say in your heart, 'Who will ascend into heaven?'[" (that is, to bring Christ down) "or 'Who will descend into the deep?'" (that is, to bring Christ up from the dead) (Romans 10:6-7, NIV)."

There should be no question in the hearts of true believers as to their salvation.

However, it is possible to be deceived. It is possible to think you are hearing from God.

That is why the Bible says this:

 "Dear friends, do not believe every spirit, but test the spirits to see whether they are from God, because many false prophets have gone out into the world (1 John 4:1, NIV)."

"For the word of God is living and active and sharper than any two-edged sword, and piercing as far as the division of soul and spirit, of both joints and marrow, and able to judge the thoughts and intentions of the heart. And there is no creature hidden from His sight, but all things are open and laid bare to the eyes of Him with whom we must give account   (Hebrews 4:12-13,NIV)."

The Bible has the final say. The truths inside are laid out plain as sight and the existence of God evident in nature so we are without excuse.

"All Scripture is God-breathed and is useful for teaching, rebuking, correcting and training in righteousness (2 Timothy 3:16, NIV)."

What do these verses mean?

"Since you have kept my command to endure patiently, I will also keep you from the hour of trial that is going to come upon the whole world to test those who live on the earth. I am coming soon. Hold on to what you have, so that no one will take your crown

(Revelation 3:10-11, NIV)."

You mean I can lose my crown-- as in I had it before and now it's gone?

"Everyone will hate you because of me, but the one who stands firm to the end will be saved (Mark 13:13, NIV)."

Are you facing persecution for standing for the Truth or are you going with the flow?

If anyone has a question in his/her mind about how meaningful having anything between you and God is, consider this!

Now a man named Ananias, together with his wife Sapphira, also sold a piece of property. With his wife's full knowledge he kept back part of the money for himself, but brought the rest and put it at the apostles' feet. Then Peter said, "Ananias, how is it that Satan has so filled your heart that you have lied to the Holy Spirit and have kept for yourself some of the money you received for the land? Didn't it belong to you before it was sold? And after it was sold, wasn't the money at your disposal? What made you think of doing such a thing? You have not lied to men but to God."

When Ananias heard this, he fell down and died. And great fear seized all who heard what had happened. Then the young men came forward, wrapped up his body, and carried him out and buried him. About three hours later his wife came in, not knowing what had happened. 8Peter asked her, "Tell me, is this the price you and Ananias got for the land?"

"Yes," she said, "that is the price."

Peter said to her, "How could you agree to test the Spirit of the Lord? Look! The feet of the men who buried your husband are at the door, and they will carry you out also."

At that moment she fell down at his feet and died. Then the young men came in and, finding her dead, carried her out and buried her beside her husband. Great fear seized the whole church and all who heard about these events (Acts 5:1-11, NIV)."

These two believers sinned by lying. They had the opportunity to repent when Peter asked them what they had done. But they didn't and dropped dead in judgment for it.

What is sin?

"If anyone, then, knows the good they ought to do and doesn't do it, it is sin for them (James 4:17, NIV)."

Adam and Eve, before they ate from the Tree of the Knowledge of Good and Evil, could only commit one sin. No other sins had been invented yet.

If there is any area of sin that is not on your conscience, provided you haven't completely hardened your heart, it is my belief you are not responsible for it until you find out.

When you have done all this, be sure to guard against pride.

"Pride goes before destruction, a haughty spirit before a fall (Proverbs 16:18, NIV)."

But if you should slip into pride for a second, do not fret, repent!

]

And last of all remember the whole entirety of 1 Corinthians 13.

To Summarize:

1.If I had all the spiritual gifts in the world, but have not love, I am nothing.

2.Love keeps no record of wrongs.

3.Love does not delight in evil, but rejoices with the truth. (So speak it even if it's unpopular!)

4.Love always hopes, always trusts, always perseveres!

<u>Obey God.</u>

Chapter 3:

Some One Sin Doctrine Reminders

Friend,

Here are some additional truths related to the "One Sin Doctrine" that I want to preserve.

1 John 1:9 (KJV)

"If we confess our sins, he is faithful and just and will forgive us our sins and purify us from all unrighteousness."

Jesus's Disciple John, addressed this verse to believers in his book, 1 John.

Even though they had committed to God initially, they still needed to continue to confess their sins to God to be continually be in a state of holiness and blamelessness.

To confess means to literally profess with your lips.

We confess out loud "Jesus is Lord" and believe that He was raised from the dead when we are saved.

We confess out loud, but only God needs to hear it, any sin we have between us and God.

I am sure you believe that God hears the prayers of His children.

Consider this verse to consider who His children are:"He that turneth away his ear from hearing the law, even his prayer shall be abomination (Proverbs 28:9, KJV)."

"If ye love me, keep my commandments (John 14:15, KJV)."

For whoever does the will of my Father in heaven is my brother and sister and mother (Matthew 12:50, NIV)."

"By their fruit you will recognize them. Do people pick grapes from thornbushes, or figs from thistles? Likewise, every good tree bears good fruit, but a bad tree bears bad fruit. A good tree cannot bear bad fruit, and a bad tree cannot bear good fruit. Every tree that does not bear good fruit is cut down and thrown into the fire. Thus, by their fruit you will recognize them. "Not everyone who says to me, 'Lord, Lord,' will enter the kingdom of heaven, but only the one who does the will of my Father who is in heaven. Many will say to me on that day, 'Lord, Lord, did we not prophesy in your name and in your name drive out demons and in your name perform many miracles?' Then I will tell them plainly, 'I never knew you. Away from me, you evildoers (Matthew 7:16-20)!'"

My question to you is how much evil does one have to do to classify it as being evil?

"Enter through the narrow gate. For wide is the gate and broad is the road that leads to destruction, and many enter through it. But small is the gate and narrow the road that leads to life, and only a few find it (Matthew 7:13-14, NIV)."

"Be perfect, therefore, as your heavenly Father is perfect (Matthew 5:48, NIV)."

Is this a command or a suggestion?

If we are already perfect in God's eyes even when we sin and "don't have to confess it," why doesn't it say this instead?

"You don't have to try to be perfect, you already are."

But no, it says to be perfect-- as in submit yourself fully to God, confessing all the sins the Holy Spirit puts on your conscience through His voice or through the Word of God.

The first conclusion that we must come to is that the Bible is completely true and that "contradictions" are just parts of the Bible we don't understand yet.

"If we deliberately keep on sinning after we have received the knowledge of the truth, no sacrifice for sins is left, but only a fearful expectation of judgment and of raging fire that will consume the enemies of God (Hebrews 10:26-27)."

We all seem to have an interpretation of what it means to have faith and experience God's grace.

A true man of faith has enough faith coupled with Holy Spirit's power to completely surrender himself. Pretty much we all did this when we were initially saved. We gave up all idolatry between us and God--- any stronghold of sin.

Sure the next day we broke God's moral law again in some areas, but we need to confess those areas. And each day we improve. Grace is unconditional forgiveness that requires us bringing our sin before God. It isn't the freedom to sin and hold onto our sin.

1 John 1:5-10 (NIV)

"But if we walk in the light, as he is in the light, we have fellowship with one another, and the blood of Jesus, his Son, purifies us from all sin. If we claim to be without sin, we deceive ourselves and the truth is not in us. If we confess our sins, he is faithful and just and will forgive us our sins and purify us from all unrighteousness. If we claim we have not sinned, we make him out to be a liar and his word has no place in our lives."

1. No one is without sin. All must first realize this.

2. However, if we confess our sins then we are purified against all unrighteousness.

3. Then, we are right before God.

In terms of salvation by faith, not by works, this is true.

It is faith that saves us, nothing we can do. For no mere man has walked in perfection his whole life and even the one sin he has committed along the way has separated him from God. It is faith and one who has faith that Jesus is Lord of his life, is in complete surrenderence to Him. He doesn't let any sin remain in his life that the Holy Spirit reveals.

However, at the same time, "faith without works is dead." Now just how much action do we need to take in obeying God? One good deed?

"But Samuel replied:"Does the LORD delight in burnt offerings and sacrifices as much as in obeying the voice of the LORD ? To obey is better than sacrifice, And to heed is better than the fat of rams (1 Samuel 15:22, NIV)."

"If you love me, keep my commands (John 14:15, NIV)."

And when we don't obey, we need to get right with God.

"What shall we say then? Shall we continue in sin, that grace may abound? God forbid. How shall we, that are dead to sin, live any longer therein (Romans 6:1-2, KJV)?"

"For if ye live after the flesh, ye shall die: but if ye through the Spirit DO mortify the deeds of the body, ye shall live (Romans 8:13, KJV)."

And in terms of grace, here's a definition you may not be familiar with:

GRACE

3. Favorable influence of God; divine influence or the influence of the spirit, in renewing the heart and restraining from sin.

My grace is sufficient for thee... 2 Cor.12

Definition from Webster's American Dictionary of the English Language, 1828.

This is far from the license to sin, but rather a soul saved by "grace" is under the influence of the Holy Spirit and thus is restrained from sin...

Under this influence, the soul can't stand to have any sin between him and God.

The following verses from one of Jesus' parables, explains falling away.

"This is the meaning of the parable: The seed is the word of God. Those along the path are the ones who hear, and then the devil comes and takes away the word from their hearts, so that they may not believe and be saved. Those on the rock are the ones who receive the word with joy when they hear it, but they have no root. They believe for a while, but in the time of testing they fall away. The seed that fell among thorns stands for those who hear, but as they go on their way they are choked by life's worries, riches and pleasures, and they do not mature. But the seed on good soil stands for those with a noble and good heart, who hear the word, retain it, and by persevering produce a crop (Luke 8:11- 15, NIV)."

Let that crop produce in you. And share the truth you know with others.

Conclusion

Life is a time of constant discovery. Do not be surprised if you learn new things each day or even discover that what you once thought to be a lie is truth. Search out a matter for yourself until you are thoroughly convinced in your own mind.

Ask God to minister to you personally and let His truths liberate you!

God Bless,

Daniel K. Arnold

Now Presenting,

The Long Awaited....

For Your Reading Pleasure and Edification...

BOOK V

CONFESSIONS OF A HEALED MAN

By
Daniel K. Arnold

Confessions of A Healed Man

Preface

This tale is real. This tale is not succinct, but written in journal-style. I am here to talk about raw Jesus Power penetrating and confounding the wisdom of this world. What is written here is nothing short of supernatural, to the glory of God.

Confessions of A Healed Man is part of a series officially preceded by The Super Hero Manual, EverChanging, Black Bird Ops, and Obey God. The first three testimonies were somewhat pleasing to the eye, somewhat talking of what itching ears want to hear. These books make up my prior testimony. They were what I knew.

Now, the cover has come off and we meet the new Daniel K. Arnold—ex-Super Hero, but still very much a Hero. Without enhancements, without psychotropic medications, Confessions of A Healed Man comes to the fore with risk and boldness. I love everyone, modeling after God who "so loved the world." Be liberated as you read! Find yourself digging deep, by "counting the cost." Find yourself submitting to the will of God no matter what challenges, trials and tribulations you face. Enjoy this book and have your life literally changed.

Find the inner hero in you!

Confessions of A Healed Man:

Chapter 1

We begin a new chapter in the life of ex-Super Hero, Daniel Arnold. He begins to find balance and dignity in Jesus Christ our Lord.

God lays him down in green pastures. He is at peace. The sedation created by man's addiction, is subsided. Daniel is alive and well praising Jesus!

This is your adventure Lord, I'm just following along. I thought it glamorous to be a Super Hero. It had its perks.

My physical enhancements, however, did not rely on the Spirit's power, but on man.

Bowing down to psychotropic pills, I was compelled to submit to the systems of this world. What would Mister Energy Plus do now or Black Bird Ops for that matter?

I sought my dignity, but the Lord asked that I seek Him. Chapter 1 of the rest of my life.

Compel Them

I am thankful for this new life. The Lord will teach me to sit still. What could I lose but life's positions? They are of honor and self-proclamation. They are of public service. But am I being healthy and spiritual?

This judgment call is finally between God and me. I know this writing is controversial, but it is real.

Who do I submit to but God? This is your decision oh Lord. Of which I will not give up. I am not sentenced to stay in the Super Hero suit. I can be liberated by the power of JESUS. This is genuine.

"Submit to God, Resist the Devil and he will flee from you." What do I want out of life, but to submit to the God that loves me!

He can set me free of any stronghold, bottom line.

His power stretches to even my impossible situation. What do I have to say to those that accuse me? The Holy Spirit will prepare me! He deserves the center of attention.

The Spirit teaches me that to rely on psychotropic medicine for my sanity is flesh. I must feed on the Word of God!

Before, psychotropic pills stopped up my ears to truth. Now, my ears are healing.

We Christian heroes of the faith, put no confidence in the flesh.

I may lose some things short-term because my fervency for Christ.

I may lose some book sales because I no longer put stock in Super Heroes, but rather the Hero— Jesus Christ.

Paul said, "I count all things but loss for the excellency of Christ Jesus my Lord: for whom I have suffered the loss of all things and do count them but dung, that I may win Christ."

To me submission to the things of God is more important than worldly dignity.

I fix my eyes on eternal matters.

Confessions of Healed Man:

Chapter 2 – Rebellion

I have rebelled against man. "The fear of the Lord is the beginning of knowledge, but fools despise wisdom and discipline." Nothing is more powerful than God. "With my God I can scale a wall."

Success lies in putting your all into victory in Jesus.

Every breath must be devoted to the truth. Before, my ears and heart seemed stopped up. Today, we must take on the truth. I must absorb it, read it, eat it.

The Bible is my survival, my food.

I may carry myself high, like I have it all together, but today the war is on! The Battle has commenced and Satan is going down. I confess victory in the name of Jesus. He is my Sure Rock that cannot be moved.

Should my life be taken, I will be with Him. For He is my stability.

I am anxious, but surely peace is here. God brings "the peace that surpasses all understanding." I want to live in that peacefully.

Truly, Happily, Genuinely.

I place my trust in the Living God who will never let me down.

What is medicine?

What is compliance?
What is change of report?

I am well and you will see that tomorrow—if I live to see the day.

Tomorrow is not promised, but today I'm following God. I do not know when my life will be required, but today and tomorrow, Lord willing, I will serve the Lord.

He is my Absolute Rock, my firm foundation. Run to Him. "Seek Him while He may be found. Call on Him while He is near."

And finally, rest.

I know I'm bucking the system and they might hate it, but I am a fighter.

"For our struggle is not against flesh and blood, but against principalities and powers in high place."

I care about the will of God and will follow to the end.

This is my ultimate adventure thus far in non-compliance to the world. To God be the glory!

God heals and He is blessing me with good health.

When anxiety tries to curtail my plans, I turn them over to God even more. Urgency begets spiritual urgency. Survival begets holding onto God. "He makes me to lie down in green pastures."

Confessions of A Healed Man:

Chapter 3

Prayer and writing help me to find my freedom. I have the urge to be purposeful in all I do.

I bet deep down you feel the same way. You want to live with a purpose. You want to have meaning in your life. You want to be at peace.

Jesus said, "My peace I give you, but not as the world gives."

What are you after, a temporary fix or an eternal communion with God? Jesus also said, "I will never leave you nor forsake you."

Stand on the promises of God and receive the Comforter, the Holy Ghost.

"He will teach you all things and bring all things to remembrance, whatsoever I have spoken unto you."

We have so much to look forwards to. We cannot fail.

"A righteous man falls down seven times and gets back up again."

I have been hospitalized over 10 times, but now my faith is truly growing.

I grow because of the Word of God and power of the Holy Ghost.

I must take a step into foreign land like Abraham. Sometimes I doubt myself. I do not have nearly as much experience as say Heidi Baker or Benny Hinn. What I have is a personal testimony of when I said YES! To God.

This is real. I have real friends who are there for me. They are the real deal and they care.

Lansing is gonna change like whoa!

Confessions of A Healed Man:

Chapter 4 – "It's Party Time"

I just cleaned my apartment some to set the scene. In the Old Testament, God ordered the people of God to throw celebrations to honor Him. People celebrated God's provision, Jehovah Jireh, God's healing, Jehovah Rophi, and other aspects of God.

Today it's Party Time for me. I have everything I need. And more!

I have real friends. Real friends do not say and do what you want all the time. Instead, they provide what is needed!

All glory be to God.

Speak the Word as it is written. Do not argue over trivial matters, but when truth counts truth counts.

"Life and death is held in the power of the tongue."

I want to speak life for myself as well as my brothers and sisters!

Confessions of A Healed Man:

Chapter 5 – Hakuna Matata

I am learning not to worry—for survival. Panic is a body reaction to high alert elements. There are times to come to the rescue and times to lay low. At all times, we should stay calm and trust in the Word.

If we can remain calm, God can better use us in emergencies. For do not want to be the walking emergency in a time that already tense.

The Bible also says there is a time for every season under Heaven. This includes mourning. It is healthy to cry our eyes out when necessary. I am learning to effectively vent to make change. God cares and we need Him to help us stay calm.

I like the song about turning our eyes upon Jesus. It fits in with the verse: "Casting all your cares upon Him for He careth for you."

We need to vent, but not primarily to man or woman. We need to vent to God, find peace and be still.

"Be still and know that I am God. I will be exalted among the nations."

Since God is in control of the large and the small, we need not worry. We need to trust.

Proverbs 3:5-8

"Trust in the Lord with all your heat. Lean not on your own understanding. In all your ways acknowledge him and he shall direct your paths. Be not wise in your own eyes. Fear the Lord and depart from evil. It shall be health to thy navel and marrow to thy bones."

I am trusting the Lord for my health. It is finished. It is complete. The work has been done.

Now we rest.

"Come to me all you who are weary and heavy-laden and I will give you rest. My burden is light; My yoke is easy."

I need the Father's rest. I need to be in the Word regularly. I need the peace of God.

Thank you Jesus my freedom has already been bought with a price.

"For he was wounded for our transgressions. He was pierced for our iniquities. The chastisement of our peace was upon him and by his wounds we are healed."

(Isaiah 53:5)

The work is complete. Now we just receive by faith. Jesus increase my faith! Hallelujah!

Confessions of A Healed Man:

Chapter 6 – Breakthrough

When you do not know what to write about, write the word "breakthrough." Pray for it. Declare it. Believe it will come to pass in the name of Jesus.

"With my God I can scale a wall." "Unless the Lord builds the house, the laborers build in vain."

We need God and we need faith. With faith, mountains move. "Get excited!"

But how do we eliminate doubt?

Keep reading saint.

You need paint to do certain types of art and you need the Bible to have material to live on, breathe on, and share.

God gave us a clean canvass. Now, be inspired to paint masterpiece by faith.

Are you bored? Are you set aside with "nothing to do?"

Pray for your passion. God has placed in you things you care about for a reason. Pursue your dreams. Write a book. Go to China. Be a spokesperson. It starts by desire and doing. Do what you dream of. Commence even if you are not talented by the world's standards. (Meet a need.)

You may very well discover who God has made you to be.

Cover responsibilities. Be dream big. Pray about it. Fast within reason of where God is leading you. Be real with yourself.

You have promise. You were made by God.

Confessions of A Healed Man:

Chapter 7 – Will Not Abandon

"You did not abandon them in the wilderness because of your great compassion

(Nehemiah 9:18-19)."

We are the People of God. He will not abandon us! Though the earth decay and our plans seem to fall apart, God will see us through if we keep the faith.

Those who have faith Obey God.

He will lead them on to victory by His (God's) standards.

"Peace I give you, but not as the world gives (Jesus)."

In times of turmoil, we must put our energy into seeking God all the more, not our worries. God has us in His hands. We can trust in Him. He gives us just enough breath for the next moment.

Confessions of A Healed Man:

Chapter 8 – On and On

I was blocked, but God blocked what blocked me. I believe it in faith. I declare it on paper. I put it in prayer. God is so real!

"God is light and in Him is no darkness at all."

When the Light shows up, the darkness has to flee. "Whom the Son sets free is free indeed." Standing before you, Oh God, is a free man. Lord do not let the devil snatch it away. Shine your light on my life and my circumstances.

I believe in Jesus. I believe He works miracles today. I believe He is doing something substantial in my life even as I write.

Tomorrow is not promised. I am going to live today and in Heaven. I heard the Lord speak, "Got this Daniel."

It is time to rest, relax and give everything to God. During times when I do not know how to escape Satan, I run to the pen of written paper, Word of God, and the face of Christ.

I express myself today Lord when I do not know just what to do. He alone rescues, saves, heals.

I worship the Living God through my gifting as all slips away around me.

All stress, anxiety, sickness, you have to flee in the name of Jesus.

He is my Rescuer. Forever and Ever Hallelujah.

I rest in the Everlasting Arm of Jesus. When I read the words God has given me I am reminded that God is a God who keeps His promises.

He has set me free!

Every hero has those moments they feel like they are in Heaven. That moment for me is now.

I napped for hours. I felt very tired and slept for six hours straight later. No night terrors. No hallucinations.

Simply waking up in peace with God's family.

"Oh Lamb of God I come."

I know who I am. These moments with God are extra special, extra glamorous. Perhaps, only He understands my bliss. Perhaps, that's the way it should be.

People may question my world. But God says he'll bring "the peace that surpasses all understanding."

Life is full of tests. Life is full of blessings. This life is temporary.

Some brothers and sisters come to rebuke us. Some come and distract us. They lack the mechanism to celebrate, but we are thankful nonetheless.

God is so in control. I love Him. He is consistent and a "rewarder of those who diligently seek after him."

I celebrate life with my Jesus. My Jesus reigns! My Jesus suffered. My Jesus is in control.

I love Jesus!

Confessions of a Healed Man:

Chapter 9 - Wise Shall Understand

Since nothing is impossible for you, from this moment forth, change me in the name of Jesus.

I know you hear me. Open up the floodgates. Let me consider not the words of man, but the very Word of God.

Move this mountain now in the name of Jesus.

Amen.

What do you want to do today Lord? It's a brand-new day. Peace is in the air for the Lord has given me perfect rest.

The people of this world cannot eliminate your truth that emanates out of the core of True Believers.

Preach your will "until the whole world hears."

Status quo, goodbye. The Lord is my Savior. I answer to Him.

Confessions of A Healed Man:

Chapter 10 – Change

We all go through mood shifts. The question is whether we hold onto the truth! Is our faith of great worth to the extent it cannot be shaken?

Would an unwarranted arrest or abuse shake us? How about the bitterness over a suicide death of a loved one? These matters are difficult to deal with but real.

Humankind lets us down, but "there is a friend that sticks closer than a brother."

That is Jesus Christ the Prince of Peace! Jesus will always be there for us through the Comforter, the Holy Ghost. Get excited. Be at peace. "Do not let your heart be troubled."

It's a brand new day.

"We walk by faith, not by sight."

Sometimes we do not know of the pitfalls that lie ahead. We need God's guidance to change our lives under unexpected tension.

Disasters happen. People die. Atrocities are committed before our very eyes. We need to be in the right place at the right time prayerfully!

"For I am convinced that neither life nor death, nor angels nor demons, nor height nor depth, nor anything else in all creation shall be able to separate us from the love of God that is in Christ Jesus our Lord (Romans 8:38-39)."

This promise is real.

"We walk by faith not by sight."

When things happen we don't like, Our God is faithful.

"For God works out all things to the good of those that love God and are called according to His purpose."

Hallelujah! Breakthrough is on its way. We need not have any fear.

"Perfect love casts out all fear because fear hath to do with torment. The man who fears is not made perfect in love."

Make me to be in your perfect love God. Draw me in and make my focus nothing or no one but you!

When I am in you, I am in bliss.

Confessions of A Healed Man:

Chapter 11 – Rebuke

I hate his rebuke, but I love the result. Truth protects me from harm.

"An honest answer is like a kiss on the lips."

It's real. It's bold. It's daring.

"Wounds from a friend can be trusted."

Wounds nonetheless hurt, but not like Hell.

"Let him know, that he which converteth the sinner from the error of his way shall save a soul from death and shall hide a multitude of sins."

(James 5:20)

Sometimes I lose my focus. That is why it is helpful for a brother or sister to help restore me. I am not on top of things all the time.

But God is and He provides the right people in my path when I need them.

In the Moment

I am resting right now in a Prayer Room. This is dessert time.

I live in the moment. Jesus is ever with me. Times are hard, but His love so bold. It never gets old. Amazing Breakthrough in this moment. I am thankful for friends, but more so thankful for your presence.

Heaven-Minded

Focusing on the eternal instead of the temporal. We are going to Heaven! Why worry about today? Let us stand together in unity in the family of God.

The family of God can be very supportive. They are your brothers and sisters after all.

With a Heaven-Minded focus we accept Godly counsel, but trust fully in the power and counsel of the Living God through the Bible.

He brings the peace that surpasses all understanding.

Confessions of A Healed Man:

Chapter 12- Round 12

Fight! Fight! Fight!

"For the weapons of our warfare are not carnal, but mighty to the pulling down of strongholds."

God pulls down strongholds and we rest. We simply let loose and let God be God.

He is in control. He <u>will</u> bless those who diligently seek after Him. He is full of grace, full of kindness. He is ready to extend His arm to you!

He cares so much for you. His heart breaks for you. He loves you like that!

The power of God changes lives. He will change you if you let Him. We have absolutely nothing to worry about when we place our trust in God.

When we know that Christ fights our battles for us, we are free to be still before God. Stillness is a beautiful thing!

Night

At the end of the day, I believe all the Lord requires of me is to relax, be quiet, and thankful for the day. There are seasons and I am exhausted.

He gives His Beloved rest as He promised. Hallelujah. Thank you Jesus. You are a blessing in my life. You are my everything.

Thank you for friends, but thank you more for being my Creator.

Simply put, I need Jesus! He is my sustenance, my very reason, and source of breathing. I live for Him.

Walking Up

It brings me greater joy than anything else to write this tale of my life.

For I was a dormant Super Hero, and now I am made alive. God is amazing the source of blessing. "How Great Is Our God."

I am watching the sun begin to rise. It's a brand-new day. This is my story. I see the Sun rising, hear the birds singing, all is well. Thank you Jesus for life. Sing with me, "How Great, How Great Is Our God."

I do not take on too much, I take on what the Lord leads me to take on; victory is in store.

"It's a beautiful day in the neighborhood (Mister Rogers)."

A new day has come. The Lord is full of blessings if we will only receive them by faith.

Super Heroes typically have enhancements to fall back on. Heroes "walk by faith, not by sight." God helps us in our infirmities. Surely we are blessed.

Today, I went on an adventure in a dentist office and I was greatly encouraged. God provided me a positive person at my side that build me up. We all need that!

As I go about my adventures in life, I remember that tension is too passing. Life is short. God is great and provides! Praise the Lord. Thank you for how you reach out to me in so many large and small ways.

Hallelujah to Jehovah Jireh, My Provider!

Transition

Under tension, under development. Waiting on the Lord, the Miracle Worker. Lord, bring me through anxiety. Keep me in perfect peace, for my mind is steadfast on you. Be my provider. Be my peace of mind in the storm. For I need you now. Help me to deal with underlying issues. You are awesome. You are in control. I love you.

I am writing this special piece that no one can take away. The Lord knows I am well.

"It is well with my soul."

I am writing a new chapter God has blessed me with and will continue bless me with for eternity. I am a man of blessing. I live a blessed life. God leads me!

"I can do all things through Christ who strengthens me."

God is my rock even when I have a headache. Life is short; life is an amazing adventure! He gives me the strength to go on. He speaks to my soul.

There are those that inspire us—that help give us the courage to go on.

These are true women and men of faith. They fight with us at our side and bless us.

I cannot ever be thankful enough for the Mariposa—the only one standing by my side right now. Thank you dear for all you've done.

Yet, the Bible is my true stability—my only rock on which I stand. Hallelujah! Jesus will never leave me nor forsake me. Hallelujah! I wait on the Lord to fill me and I am at peace. Provide "justice against my adversaries" and "forgive for they know not what they do."

Confessions of A Healed Man:

Chapter 13- New Chapter

There is peace in the name of Jesus. He brings the peace that surpasses all understanding. I am thankful for my God who reaches out to me and through the brethren!

I am fellowshipping right now. The Lord works in mysterious ways. Thank you Jesus. It's a brand-new day and I'm alive to hear the birds. I reached out to a brother last night. I just met him last night.

"God works out all things to the good of those who love him and are called according to his purpose."

God is good. He is faithful and will bring us through the storm even if we have to stand alone like the prophets or like Noah. God will bring us through if we are faithful. Thank God for another day. Hallelujah!

I am deep in the trenches at CMH. I no longer belong to this organization. I am affiliated based on employment that may be taken away. It was short-term anyhow. God is great! He provides for my every need. I am here for a reason. I am sure. "There are no accidents (Kung Fu Panda)."

And there are no accidental people.

God blesses us right where we are and lifts us up out of the muck. I am thankful for a good God.

His Word does not return void, but accomplishes what He desires (Isaiah 55).

I want to be a part of His Plan. I want to make a difference. I desire to touch lives. Lord, use me, despite how difficult this road may be.

Thank you!

Waiting

I wait upon the Lord for breakthrough. I know He is faithful. Breakthrough happens when we least expect it, but we be ready!

God wants to spring to life at the bountiful opportunities He gives us. Hallelujah! We wait expectantly for miracles to breakout. The Lord is ever-faithful, ever-true, never giving up on us!

Oh what a "Happy Day" that Jesus has paid the price for our freedom. This freedom is real. "It is well. It is well with my soul."

The cool breeze blows in the hot sun. God is in the midst of chaos. I know I am surely blessed. He led me out and I went. I thank God for you and need to consider you in my prayers. Surely, you are a blessing to me, cheering up my mood like the sun.

"The power of your love is changing me." You are an incredible God. I witness so many miracles today. I "walk by faith not by sight." This is incredible. I am making new friends and doing Kingdom Building. God is incredible!

"Anticipate great things." A quote my Dad said that was really encouraging!

God works things out—"without a doubt." Yeah!

Praise the Lord! He is working things out!

I am like food cooking on the stove, weird analogy yes. I am being cooked to precision for your purpose. It hurts sometimes, but God has a master plan. He's transforming my heart!

Thank you Jesus!

I am having a lot of trouble sleeping. I trust in the Lord to bring me through or bring me home.

I love the Lord. He gives me a sound mind. He is my stability. Thanks be to God for every breath of life.

Jesus died and rose from the dead and so have I. I was once dead in my transgressions, but now I am alive in Christ!

Hallelujah! New Life! "On earth as it in in Heaven. I do not have to wait any longer. I live an operate in paradise. I am truly liberated. "No more shackles. No more chains. I am free (Mary, Mary, Musical Artist)."

Confessions of A Healed Man:

Chapter 14 - Going On

What do you want to do today? "All things are possible with God." I know I am here for a reason and a season. Jesus lead on. Life with you is blessed!

The Spiritual Body is like a great orchestra. Subtlety as well as boldness are both profound. There must be a balance and a conductor. Variety of instruments, notes , volume and tempo are all integral. There must be unity and love for music and each other.

I have been healed and the Lord is not afraid, for He is God. He is profound.

I am learning how to rebuke the devil.

Recipient Rights

Take three with you to plead your case. To remember that God is with you, Father, Son, Holy Ghost."

"You're going to that appointment Daniel."

Acts of Nature I've never seen before.

Surreal and Tree Animals.

Let your words be seasoned with grace.

"And all the trees of the field shall clap their hands (Isaiah 55)."

"Do not worry about what man can do to the body," but do not scare man either.

"Charity is not puffed up."

Strangers

When we entertain strangers, we entertain angels unaware.

God has brought a special person to me right tonight. He has brought his presence through an imperfect person.

Words that come out of the pen can be hard to communicate in the heat of the night. God directs and brings stillness. He is absolutely in control.

One Miracle at a Time

Believe

Bless

Repeat

I am thankful for being alive. Life is a life of adventure, trials, and love. If my mind is a job, God is the Boss.

"He calls the shots, I follow!"

I wake up in the morning and head to the local drop-in center. God is good and in Him is no darkness at all.

Who is completely good but God alone? No one.

I testify to the power of the Living God. There is a lot of tension here, but God is still in the midst.

I am praying for thirstiness. Hallelujah!

Platform

Today, I retract everything but Jesus. I speak boldly of his love and faithfulness as experienced in my life!

God is very real.

I need your strength to continue. I cannot do this by myself. I cannot coast. I need your strength right here in this place because mine is not working.

Day after day I pine for sleep and the world criticizes me. Many people doubt me and that is among the few I have entrusted.

Oh Lord, be my rescuer! "Save" me "from the fowler's snare and from the deadly pestilence."

I do not want to be a Super Hero; I want to be your hero walking "by faith not by sight."

Oh Lord, I cry out to you. Increase my faith today in the name of Jesus. You are beautiful. You are all I care about.

I would die for you, but I'd rather live and proclaim the goodness of God. Hallelujah!

I've burned my cart and roasted my oxen. There is no turning back. Take all of me.

Amen. In the Name of Jesus. The Name above all names.

In my weakness, be my strength, Jehovah Jireh! Hallelujah!

You are my God. I place all my trust in you!

I believe you will make this happen. I give my life right here. Take me, all of me! He gives His Beloved Res

Confessions of A Healed Man:

Chapter 15 – Rest

Some may sleep. Some may slumber. Many will never enter His rest.

"He who places His trust in Him will never be put to shame."

I will fight to the end! I am not joking. I am not conceited. I am living a full life. Do not pity me no matter what the world says the result is.

Jesus is my God. He is my sufficiency!

You deserve all the glory for bringing me safe thus far.

"Every man dies. Not every man really lives (Braveheart, Movie)."

I am thankful for this life, but I am ready to go. I want to keep living and make a dent, yet I know my true home is in Heaven.

"They may take our lies, but they will never take our freedom (Braveheart, Movie)!"

I am living out my purpose right now and it is exciting!

"What should it profit a man if He should gain the entire world yet forfeit his soul (Jesus)."

Jesus lived it out in 33 years. I've had longer than that, but spent many years sedated, drugged, squelched.

With the grace of God I have been given this time to truly live!

Lord, if the day comes that I am drugged again, I hang onto the Word of the Lord.

"We drank poison and did not die (Bible)."

I am not against medicine, but psychotropic brain re-adjustment. I am against forced sedation because of lack of faith.

Jesus paid the price for my wrongdoing and my health. I stand on His promises alone, bottom line.

It's a new day! We are walking "by faith, not by sight."

We may lose worldly positions. We may be chained up metaphorically. We may be forced to go places we do not want to go, but Jesus is faithful! He will lead us to Glory Land. He will bring satisfaction. He is the rock on which we stand.

There is a new, challenging adventure every day. Let's embrace it!

Let's change the world with our lives by living out wholeheartedly while we are alive, no compromise!

Confessions of A Healed Man:

Chapter 16 - Fear

There is nothing to fear because God is near! He is fully in control, around us, and in us.

"If our God is for us, who could be against us."

Turn your requests over to the God that answers prayer. It is not good to demand things for man when God is the one who makes a way.

Hallelujah.

Jesus frees us. He brings us fresh insight and a new life. Live the adventure of the hero today!

Be motivated to live a changed life by turning over everything over to Jesus!

I like life, but life does not always like me, for I am not of this world.

I have trouble sleeping at night, but it is an opportunity to worship God.

"God works out all things to the good of those who love Him and are called according to His purpose."

I know my God is faithful, even if I should stumble. HE will not let me down—ever.

"For God so loved the world that He gave His one and only Son that whosoever believeth in Him shall not perish but have eternal life."

This life given is as it says. It lasts forever! It is time to live it up to the fullest forever and ever.

Why do I write with repetition? It is my meditation to remind myself of God's faithfulness. I am thankful for Him and will document His miracles as healing is upon me!

"For God did not give us a spirit of fear, but of power, of love and of a sound mind (2 Timothy 1:7)."

Not of This World

We are "not of this world" so why should we seek after the acceptance of this world?

God has a special plan for all of us. He cares for ever hair on our heads. "We are worth more than many sparrows."

We can go on because our support system in God always goes on! Praise the Lord.

Dream

I would most wish to have this manuscript published and combined with previously published manuscripts. It is my dream to reach the far corners of the earth with the love of Jesus through writing.

Lord, bring this to pass!

I desire it more than riches, a wife, prosperity. Let people be liberated in the name of Jesus.

Jesus is in control and His ways are beautiful and kind. He is perfect and we are not. He is faithful.

I love Jesus!

Confessions of A Healed Man:

Chapter 17 - Taking Off the Mask: Embracing Healing by the Power of Jesus

I am in bliss today. I am relaxing volunteering in a front desk position. The Lord is bring peace to a typically chaotic surrounding. All glory be to God.

I love being helpful and relaxing at the same time. God giving me awareness of my surroundings.

There is peace in the House today! I am so amazed, so blessed. "I waited on the Lord and He heard my cry." He answered me and brought blessing not a curse!

With His Spirit, He gives a perfect answer to everything, I am just a conduit.

When I do not know how to react, I model appropriate behavior.

I am overwhelmed with blessing right now. I do not know how long it will last, I am in Heaven right now at this very moment.

"Jesus is Lord."

I am not here to control the place, just to be a chaperone of peace.

Confessions of A Healed Man:

Chapter 18 – Resting Quotes

I am not perfect, but God is and I represent Him as best I can.

I may be on fire today but God is on-fire everyday and after I pass He will continue to be on-fire.

When you serve your enemies, it heaps burning coals on their heads that are actually soothing!

I do not have the authority to enforce things unless I'm an employee. But I can make a difference! ☺

Whew.. The devil may be working overtime, but God is still the Boss.

I just held down the fort for a second. Excitement, suspense.

Relax, I'm not in control. (God is.)

Smile at your enemies (with love).

Recognize faces, names, and smile. #Respect

Observe potential calamities and respond (if you can) before they happen.

Every part of a machine is necessary. Just like the Body of Christ.

Acknowledging the unacknowledged is beautiful.

Sometimes I have control issues.

God gives us more freedom than anyone and He is in control.

I need a break. I know God will provide. He is awesome like that.

Being in control is not important.

Goal: 'Til 4, to show I'm capable!

God has an answer for everyone. Just ask the Holy Spirt! Yeah!

Jesus sees everything.

I am truly healed. This is the best day of my life. It was worth all previous turmoil.

God knows the perfect dose of natural stuff. #ModerationInEverything

Awesome! God calmed down this whole place.

God loves these people.

I am learning to!

Love is damage control.

It's not against the rules to raise your hands. #praisebreak!

DKA 6/15/16

God sees the potential in you. Do you?

When in need, press your plea. God answers prayer!

Encouragement comes of my mouth by the Spirit, I almost can't control it.

Operating in the gifts. Whoa! Whoa!

Jesus runs the show and He makes us look GOOD.

Even if you are a great conductor, you still need the instruments and musicians. #ValueTheBody

First impressions set a tone.

Smile if you don't know what to say.

A great way to love is to try not to offend unless you need to and then be gentle.

Frequently: Do not say what you are going to do, just take initiative.

You could learn a lot from a humbled out person. #TakeNotes

Confessions of A Healed Man:

Chapter 19 – More Resting Quotes

When you don't know what to do, look up!

His love outshines earthly love and affection.

Beautiful Minds require a lot of work.

Let the inspiration come when it comes! Until then, rest and pray.

It's hard to keep track of 100 people. #Delegation

Acknowledgement: I need help!

Showcase others' contributions, besides your own.

Not everything has to be perfect. That is where unique creativity comes in.

Do not misuse Scripture even if what you communicate sounds catchy.

My brain may be full, but I am not supposed to carry the message by myself.

I am aware of many things, but I report emergencies and urgencies.

I am not a dictator so I don't point out everything.

#NotMyJob

If you feel you always have to say something, you may have a control issue.

Let God take care of it.

Document your miracles.

If praise is neglected, do share it at the time of need.

Enjoy life. Cherish Heaven.

Wait for the appointed hour.

Let people vent their anger and react only when necessary.

Diversions have their place.

People like to hear: "You just made my day in a unique way!"

Encouragement is as necessary as rebuke.

The center of attention is stressful to everyone but God. #DestresswithJesus

If you are instrumental in changing even one life, you've begun your job.

Sometimes it's difficult to smile.
#MournWithThoseWhoMourn

It is a miracle that I am not overwhelmed right now.

It's a labor of love, because it doesn't pay very much.

Addiction: Turn a need, into a want, into the trash. #GodHelpUsAll

This awakening is the best day of my life so far.

You cannot regulate things. So don't fret. #WeNeedGod

It may not be breakdown season, but rather rebuilding season.

Sometimes it's good to keep your mouth shut: Observe, Record, Document, Share.

Selah. Even when you are doing your favorite things, break are required on earth.

The best break is keeping your mouth shut.

I like the way you take your time, it says I'm in charge of myself.

Beautiful minds need maintenance.

"The buck stops here." Sometimes the only break is a praise break when it's hectic.

I want to say even if it was just for a day, I really lived my life.

You don't need to too your own horn. People will toot the truth in some manner.

Can't do it all by myself.

(I am having difficulty enduring this shift.)

Communication is very crucial. You are very crucial. Do you part.

Legalism is not necessary.

If you want to be respected, do not make a joke out of everything.

Intentional people do not utter everything on their minds.

Leave bombs alone unless you are ready "to take one for the team." #CountingTheCost

Not every moment of victory is glamorous.

Leaders spend time alone.

Take a break from working on your masterpiece. You may be inspired.

"Drinking is a matter of life or death." ~James

"That drinking had to go, it's a matter of life and death." ~James

Thank you God for moving on my church.

Your Spirit is here.

I do not want to simply ask, "What is my job?" I want to be in my destiny.

We are here in the park again where you confounded the wise and brought peace to this man of misery.

You "work out all things to the good of those that love you and are called according to your purpose."

Just because you do not understand, does not mean I'm crazy. #SoundMind

Stress pushes us to trust in God or "take the bait of Satan.

Confessions of A Healed Man:

Chapter 20: 6/17/16

I am thankful for life. I am still alive. I am still free. God is in control. He is giving me responsibility and favor. He is a good Lord.

When things go down and there is fear, Christ uses us to shine the Light of the Father.

"What man meant for evil, God meant for good."

My private life is strictly on a needs to know basis. #"OnAMissionFromGod"

"Don't throw your pearls before swine." Give them to future kings and queens.

A good rule of thumb is to sip on your provision, not gourge it down in five seconds.

Work it. Rest it. Get it done. #AlltotheGlory

Do not privately confess negative feelings. Give it to God and smile and praise. #TheTruth

It is good to have the faith to do all things, but it is important to focus on your calling from God.

Focus. Only God knows everything.

The best way to lose anxiety is to not worry about tomorrow, but take care of today's needs. #WithGod'sHelp

It's about souls not products. If you love the customer, they come back to buy everything in the store just to see your face. #Love

You open up my eyes with your Holy Spirit.

I'm in my prime right now. I'm living my life better than I ever have.

Encourage the brethren.

Sometimes you just need to get up and walk around.

I was not placed on this earth to check people out and be flesh. #Purity

Encourage your brothers and sisters despite infirmity.

Not every day floats by easily or equally. There are blessed moment, tender moments, and rip-roaring difficult moments.

We need the Body, but if we are abandoned on earth, we have God Himself.

In the park, I dwell. I lay down and listen, tuning into the voice of God.

It is almost unbearable to lie awake here most of my life, keeping the night terrors at bay.

God is good, all the time.

Help me Jesus to cope. Give me a tremendous day of breakthrough. "Tomorrow is not promised". Bliss is great, but perhaps a day of trusting leaning and growing is even better.

Hallelujah!

It's such a hard burden to bear. I'm glad life He bears it for me.

As I fight to sleep by faith and peace, the world hates me. People of God criticize me.

I feel a worm of a man, but I know there is a silver lining and "we walk by faith not by sight."

I know someone out there is growing faith by this writing that God has placed in me.

Someone about to commit suicide is changing their mind by the power of Jesus.

I am not suffering in vain. There is hope. "Though the sorrow may last for a night, His joy comes in the morning!"

Endure hardship my friends and know that there are those mourning with you. You will go on!

I pray for you now as you read this book. Jesus help the broken, children of the Lord. Save a life. Be an inspiration. "Do not let your hearts be troubled." Bless everyone reading this in the name of Jesus!

Take a walk. Make a good decision.

Someone who was going to do something foolish just changed their mind.

God is good!

I have this hunger to reach out and help someone even if it's just me.

Do you know how hard it is to stay awake most of the night, contemplating good health and wake up happy in the morning and be criticized for it?

To enjoy moments of God's faithfulness and be called manic, when you know you are waking "by faith not by sight."

"God is faithful. He will not allow you to be tempted beyond what you can bear, but will provide a way escape through Christ Jesus our Lord."

Jesus changing my heart for the better, even in the heartache. We are the Body. We are Ever Changing from glory to glory.

When we suffer, the whole Body suffers. Let us in turn "mourn with those who mourn."

I cannot blame the status of this body on meds. I am not taking them. I am relying on Jesus. Should I die tonight or sometime soon, do not pity me.

For I am fully living my life. I am happy. I am joyous! WHOA! Pity the man or woman who lives a lukewarm life. This life is short. Serve God and take joy in the toil.

We are here to serve!

"It's a great day to be alive."

Wait on the Lord. For He hears our cry. "We shall mount up with wings as eagles. We shall run and not be weary."

God has provided a wearing, willing soul as I request He is using my wakefulness to the glory of God right now.

Save this man from hellfire tonight. Break all his vices now, as we speak in the name of Jesus.

Moods change. They fluctuate. Even the pen I communicate with does not behave at times. Does that mean I give up? Never!

Love finds a way. Callings are birthed and will be implemented.

In this journey, confessions bring life and death. "Life and death is held in the power of the tongue." I will not lose heart. I will press on.

"I will not die, but live and declare the works of the Lord."

At times, that provision shows up at the last possible moment.
This too is to the glory of God. He shows His glory in miraculous provision.

"It is good to worship and praise the Lord."

It is a season of close friends that are there for us. Still watch out for "wolves in sheep's clothing." They can be close too.

Jesus give me discernment.

If you are devoted to Christ, when the going gets tough, breakthrough is on its way. #JesusIsUnbreakable

You are a work in progress. Your story is just being lived out. People are reading, but you are not here for them first. To God be the glory for real.

"You were bought with a price. Therefore, honor God with your body."

Rest is being content regardless of whether I have 100 years to live or 15 minutes. #Trust

Rest is intimacy with the Father.

Serving the Lord is not just surviving, it's seeing abundance in God's blessings in your life. #Purpose

I couldn't have done it without the Body. #MiraclesCanHappen

Never leave your wingmen in a spiritual corner.

Focus is important.

"Do not be drunk on wine, but be filled with the Holy Spirit."

Play outside of your head—in the Spirit.

This ministry was worth everything. Jesus give me the willingness to give my life to save a life. "

Miracles can happen to those who love the Lord."

In the morning, I wake up and serve the Lord. This journal is to the glory of God. I want to be more filled with love, for this is pleasing to the Lord.

I am here for others in need, but more here for God.

When we do not know what to do, we wait on the Spirit.

Physical death is inevitable, but so is new life for believers.

I am not trying to be rude;

I am being natural and organic.

I really believe what I'm talking about.

I am not trying to provoke wrath,

I am being myself.

Tune into the Spirit.

Counseling can happen in the midst of entry-level service. #BlessedBeyondImagination

No use rushing the inspiration. God meets our spiritual needs in the now!

Give an honest answer even if it's embarrassing.

Confessions of A Healed Man:

Chapter 21 – The "Nitty Gritty"

I will give a corporate testimony of forsaking life all to the glory of God.

(You're going to bring faith to this whole building.)

I am going to India someday.

Revival in JIMHO

INTERCESSION

All the way!

The almost sacrifice of Isaac—willingness to "go the distance."

A year from now! Testimony 6/05/16-6/05/17

"No eye has seen, no ear has heard, what God has prepared for them that love Him.

I am (His)free!

Help me to see the potential in <u>everyone</u>.

I am an Apostle.

He gives me a beautiful mind. The devil cannot steal it away!

The anointing is on me. God extends it to me even when my earthly infirmities make me feel weak. I cope, through "the author and perfecter of my faith."

He endured so much in an earthly body as a model to me. I shall make it through the fire. In the meantime, "by His stripes I am healed!"

"Bless the Lord oh my soul and all that is within me."

Every part of me belongs to God. He is liberating me more every day as I submit to Him.

I am thankful for His faithfulness.

Right now, I feel the tension; I feel the warfare. It comes like a storm, but I know God will pull me through.

"We walk by faith not by sight." We fix our eyes on Jesus and determine not to lose heart, remembering His commitment to us. Praise the Lord!

This is my season of rest and volunteering. Breakthrough is here and will continue to manifest.

Lord keep me focused—on-point. I am easily distracted. I easily fall into worldliness.

We are in the flesh, but the Spirit resides in us. Following the Spirit makes anything possible—like changing the world one sector at a time.

God is the only one who can change everything at once. We are along for the ride—one focus at a time—making a dent one day at a time.

We are parts of the Body and need each other. And apart from Jesus, we can do nothing.

Thank you Jesus for the opportunity to be myself and serve you and love you.

Life is amazing like that!

Confessions of A Healed Man:

Chapter 22 – Power Quotes

I find meaning in public service—especially when I share the love of God at the same time. #Freedom

Specialization: Unique Gifting

Investment, Love, Focus

Apply yourself, but do not overstretch yourself. Play your part, not God's. You are not meant to be a dictator.

Do not give up when you are in the desert, because you are developing patience, roots, and depth.

Use as many diverse communication techniques as possible to as best as possible accommodate everything. #NoOneLeftBehind

You actually inspire others with your modesty. Don't give up.

Consider your every word. You want people to know something important coming whenever you talk.

Be considerate of others' cultures in love.

Your positive energy is craved even when we do not smile back.

"In the Spirit of the Lord, there is freedom."

Love can be scattershot or direct, as long as it's genuine.

Accommodation is empathetic, understanding, love and of course flexible.

How can I encourage people the most? Be consistent over time.

Inspiration comes when we need it, not necessarily when we want it.

Lord, show me how to reach all the hurting people—especially those who hate me. Let me not give up. Give me strength, in the name of Jesus, Amen!

Do not worry about when others prevail and you seem to be left lacking. God is faithful. You will have your day.

Bringing "hope to the hopeless."

I am here to love everyone right where they are as an imitator of Christ.

Ingenuity is required under the duress of life's struggles. "Love finds a way!"

You are important to us!

It is an honor to know my enemies feel comfortable being in the same room as me. Therefore, I am joyous. There is hope and His name is Jesus!

The wisest answer may be dismissed in the presence of bitterness, but if you are speaking in pure love, do not relent.

Breakdown the strongholds, by your power Jesus.

Faithfulness shows up even when things look bleak.

You may leave your legacy the most when things look hopeless.

We shouldn't walk on pins and needles when our enemy is in the room; we should see opportunity.

No matter what someone says, positive or negative, our actions and investment show what we believe.

Scattershot or point blank, love is still love! #MakeADifference

As heroes, opportunities to smile and see blessings can be so abundant they are overwhelming. #Overflow #Share #Repeat

People like to consume food in diverse ways. The same is true for receiving truth.

It's best not to wait for emergencies. Rebukes can be as painful as having an I.V. put in your arm to receive food.

Humans let us down, God never will let us down.

Just persist in your love. #ExpectNothingInReturn

We can all reach different people. That's what makes us different.

People sometimes get under your skin to see if you are made of love!

In the Spirit we need not be offended. ("Our struggle is not against flesh and blood."

Happiness is knowing your assignment is to help people smile!

Never become too busy for your friends, but do not neglect work either.

When you feel like panicking, give thanks. Your patience muscles are being worked out!

No one who is breathing is completely disabled. #Empowerment

People who let go of fear have better reasoning skills.

We are meant to overcome adversity, not avoid it.

There's almost nothing I desire more than to work surrounded by the sick in the presence of the Healer. #Jehovah Rophi

Multiple Minds = More Creativity

People love chaos when they feel empowered to change things!

Quote: Most people want the opportunity to say what's on their mind.

It is better to bring a sinner to repentance than to snitch on him/her.

It is better to snitch on a suicidal person than let them die in suicide.

I am not nearly as talented as the Holy Spirit inside me.

Even your worst enemy needs encouragement.

Fellowship opportunities do not always come at the most ideal times. #SeizeTheDay

Some people sit around idle all day complaining, when they are meant to reach out to others in worse circumstances.

Not everyone understands tears of joy!

I'm living my dreams when I see the broken learn to smile!

Do not worry about your joy being stolen in the future. Focus on praising God for the joy now!

We all need praise breaks...

If this place ripped out into total chaos, our people skills could not save us, only God could intervene. #NothingWithoutHim

The 2nd Day of Paradise is sweeter than the day before because it's consistency.

Youthfulness knows no age boundary.

When God inspires people and they share His love, His Spirit blows stronger than a fierce tempest.

When you give people the space that they need, you give them more room to love you.

I am in Heaven, want to come join me? #FreelyYouHaveReceivedFreelyGive

Your enemies keep you around when you become indispensable because of His love!

Love isn't afraid to smile even though he/she may be punch in the face for it.

Do not stifle your smile when people want to see you frown with them. #BeTheMiracle

Some people are truly liberated.

Serve and you will be served.

Secret Bonus Book:

Still Breathing

Chapter 1

I am alive. I am breathing. I am better than before. I am blessed.

I have been institutionalized 60 of the previous 90 days.

I will never retract my faith. This commitment is to the death!

Literally. I love my life. I will leave a legacy. Rock on!

I have seen things, done things, lived my life.

I am ready for Heaven; every day is like Heaven.

"To live is Christ, to die is gain."

I love my life. I love you, everybody. Life is incredible! Wowee...

A whole new world!

I am still alive!

Look around you; find out that life is incredible!

We are surely blessed.

Get excited. God has a plan for you and for me.

Are you willing to kick it out into 100% and run that race as to get the prize?

Life can be so incredible.

"All things are possible with God!"

I am thankful for you.

If you are reading this right now, know that I am in a good place, taken care of.

I may disappear off the grid, but it is to the glory of God!

It is time to rest and rejuvenate. It is time to breathe in and out Jesus Christ!

It is time to stop playing games and walk in the Spirit.

It is time to be satisfied "as with the richest of foods."

It is time to walk in freedom.

I am in Bridges Crisis Unit right now loving my life. God is awesome!

Enjoy restrictions. Concentration Camps allow you to specialize, to love on your guards and take care of co-prisoners.

God is good all the time.

Get excited about life.

God has made you to have fun! To find pleasure in the daily toil because when you give life your best, you are serving a Heavenly Master!

Rock on Batman!

"God works out all things to the good of those who love Him and are called according to His purpose."

You have a purpose. You are all so beautiful.

Live to your potential like whoa!

Woohoo! "There are no accidents (Kung Fu Panda)."

You were made special, amazing.

Call me Manic, but I want to be able to say with every breath that I love you,

That Jesus loves you.

Live this life 100%. Woohoo!

God is great! Life is just plain awesome.

"On earth as it is in Heaven (The Lord's Prayer)!"

I am stoked. I am saved. I am plentiful!

I love you. I miss my JIMHO!

Justice in Mental Health Organization!

I am committed to God. He has me. Not a thousand needles full of Haldol could ever stop that!

I am in this to the end. I love my life!

I remember encouragement from Ed the Nurse at White Pine Behavioral Hospital.

God's got me. He will take care of me for always!

Know that God is real. Call out to Him and experience God today.

"Forever and ever, Hallelujah!"

I rest in the Lord from now to never end.

Do you know what eternity means in Heaven?!

It is the bliss of all bliss. It is the euphoria screaming out of my head—the goodness of Jesus!

Jesus!

Yes. Yes. Yes.

Tell me I'm on a Manic trip, like Mozart when he wrote Handel's Messiah!

Oh Jesus, you are so awesome.

I took a needle from the Anti-Christ system, been committed recently for over 60 days.

Now, I am free. You've released me from the grip.

You've freed me to take the pills. No more Haldol torture!

God is amazing like that.

I comply for now. In Heaven, I do the freedom dance.

Right now, I am in total bliss.

Let me praise the King with every breath I have.

Book it, write your story down.

God is amazing, powerful and so in love with His Church!

Hallelujah!

In Babylon, Jesus reigns. In famine, darkness or storm, Jesus reigns in me.

Do you know what it is like to be forced into what you don't believe in?

Do you know what it is like to put your faith in God and still be needle-pushed?

God will bring me through. He is <u>my</u> Lord.

He loves me to the death! "Amazing love, how can it be?"

I do not come with the analytical wisdom of the world, but with the powerful boldness of Jesus.

Search a matter out. Be free today!

This is probably not my final hurrah.

For I am free today even writing to you today in the middle of the night in this beautiful crisis unit.

Oh my God!

Oh my God!

Glorify thy name in all the earth!

4:47am

10/12/16

Enjoy your life, Serve Jesus!

☺

Life is not over for you!

Enjoy every moment!

To the end!

To the death!

"To die is gain."

Whoa! Hallelujah. This is Heaven!

I am ecstatic. I am delighted.

My name is Daniel. It means, "God will be my Judge."

God surely knows my heart.

I make mistakes but God is for me for eternity.

Daddy Jesus got my back. Rock on!

This is my capstone. This is my life's story. Obey God today!

I have really messed up. I have pulled three fire alarms in my life, in three different places.

I have been evil. I have been filled with selfishness and lust.

But God has forgiven me by grace.

"I am free!"

I have five scheduled days in the Crisis Unit. I can write every night if I choose by going to bed at 6pm!

God is amazing. He got my back like whoa.

God is so real. Turn to Him while there still is time.

I guess I am a writer and there is no chance in Hell of stopping me.

"We're not gonna take it anymore (Twisted Sister)!"

God is so amazing!

Yes. I am in Heaven right now!

Relaxing with Jesus. ☺

The bliss of Jesus is UNSTOPPABLE!

Am I having a false Charismatic moment or do I really know Jesus has me for all eternity?

Rest in peace forever. Rest in peace while you are alive.

Rest in peace in shackles!

"Take these shackles off my feet so I can dance (Mary Mary)!"

But if these shackles remain, to God be the glory!

God has me!

Really, really.

As you wish Christ, I will proceed.

This is an amazing life. I will say, I have lived life to the fullest!

Take me Jesus, take me now!

Into the Heavenly of Heavenlies!

Today, I decide to rest forever. Jesus has me like that!

"Get excited (Jason Arnold)."

I may be on a night watch, but God has and will be watching me for all eternity.

He is the Alpha and Omega. The beginning and the end. Who can understand the world of a non-compliant crazy?

Someone who rebels to the very end.

I love my Jesus. He will really see us through any storm—even if it seems we have to walk like Peter on water.

Rock on world!

Super Heroes are real.

I am so free.

This is my miracle time with Jesus.

Writing my story under supervision.

Am I an Animaniac?

I don't know. You tell me.

Should I join the Goof Troop? I think I already have.

Rock on this beautiful life with Jesus!

I have been a real rebel, both good and bad.

I've upset the apple cart but Jesus forgives!

Yes!

Take me Jesus, take me now to the next adventure!

You are amazing, steady never changing.

You are my stability.

Rest in Jesus now, really. Take a break from your anguish and run with Jesus!

I didn't know the next step. "For we walk by faith not by sight!"

Let go right now. Ask God if there is anything between Him and you. Get yourself together. Go the extra mile.

Don't be legalistic, be free! God wants to communicate with you PERSONALLY. "If we confess our sins, He is faithful and just to forgiveth our sins and to cleanse us from all unrighteousness (I John 1:9)."

It's that simple. It's that easy. Now go and sin no more! Hallelujah!

We have an advocate in the court of God.

Jesus!

Still Breathing

Chapter 2 – Thankfulness

I am thankful for you, for all you do!

Your love is grand Jesus and all my friends.

Life is beautiful! Never give up.

Don't give up! Run with God hardcore!

Woohoo!

Be a peaceful radical, never ever let up!

Thank you Jesus for awesome friends!

Rest in Jesus right now. Take a break. Selah. A musical rest. God is so good.

Give Him five minutes of silence of listening of peaceful pause.

Don't look back. God has a destiny for us, "Something Beautiful."

Wow! You have so much potential to be a world-changer!

Thank you all my great friends who take the time to care for me.

You are awesome. Give your hearts to Jesus and
go the extra mile!

Yeah!

Still Breathing

Chapter 3 – Rest

Rest is possible. Rest is sublime. Rest has calming features.

Jesus said, "Come to me all you who are weary and heavy-laden and I will give you rest. My burden is light and my yoke is easy."

Rock on Jesus!

Let us be at peace, "both now and forever."

Jesus was awake on the night of His betrayal.

From this I gather that rest is more than sweet sleep. It is "the peace of God that surpasses all understanding."

Do not worry your wee head if you miss some sleep spending time with the Savior.

Rest in Jesus. Do not panic. "Be still and know that I am God. I will be exalted above the nations."

Try to sleep, but if you don't praise God no matter what!

Rock on! This is freedom. This is love. This is living the jubilant life!

Still Breathing

Chapter 4 – Storyteller

I have been very evil. The past is over so why re-live it with storytelling.

It is time to glorify God with my mouth.

The mouth in the Book of James is like the rudder of a ship.

We must choose our words carefully—to glorify the Lord and not past sin.

I repent, Lord help me!

I find my peace in Jesus. Oh Father help me!

Tell good stories that humbly bring glory to God!

For example: My best personal advocacy resulted in a typed letter from a nurse manager. I took action through Recipient Rights while I was in confinement.

"All things are possible with God!" "There are no accidents."

Thank you Jesus!

This is a great story and it helped the little guy.

Jesus cares for the little guy. "Whatever you do unto the least of these brethren you do unto me (Jesus, Bible)."

He look out for His children and rewards those who diligently seek after Him.

Be a storyteller for God. Give a testimony whenever you can. Glorify the things of God, not evil!

Who are we serving, the devil or God?

I have so much to learn. God help me and pray for me too.

"Glorify thy name in all the earth."

Still Breathing

Chapter 5 – Downtime

Everyone needs their own private downtime, stripped of stimulation.

This is where I am willing or not willing.

I am stripped of busyness for the time being, but I can write to you.

I can pray too. "Life is good."

This is a time I can dream big. Things are better than I could've imagined. I thought my destination was Adult Foster Care.

Soon, I will be released to frolick in my own apartment. I will have a beautiful time as much as now is beautiful.

Life with Jesus is cool, even in the downtime.

Thank you Jesus!

I want to become an international Evangelist, but right now I have Lansing to work with.

Praise the Lord for His beautiful work!

Still Breathing

Chapter 6 – Insomnia!

Here I walk the hall all night long. I take a break to talk to you, my reading friends.

I will "make the most of every opportunity for the days are evil."

I wish I was asleep, but here I am for your reading pleasure!

Praise the Lord! I love you all. You are special to me—every last one of you.

Thank you all your great friends in my life!

There is rest for those who rest in Jesus. It is eternal. It cannot be measured. It is "the peace that surpasses all understanding."

Resting in the Lord is beautiful!

I have absolutely nothing to worry about. God is faithful.

"I have a home in Heaven (J. Brian Craig)."

"We walk by faith not by sight."

Still Breathing

Chapter 7 -The Beautiful Life

Do not ever give up on the life Jesus has for you!

Sound the trumpet; do not withhold the most sincere praise. Imagine and know breakthrough now. Savor the moment. Live every breath for JESUS!

He is the Liberator. I am His servant. There is loyalty there, but I have wronged Him in so many ways.

He never quits on me. He is my Lord and Savior. I want to be loyal to Him to my last breath and then eternity united with the Savior.

Do you want an eternity of bliss? It's an awful lot like life right now for me!

Moment by moment is gorgeous right now!

Pure awesome. He the Lord is with me right now in my heart. No one can take that away.

No one! Yes, freedom!

Freedom over me, in me and all around.

Bliss is here in the midst of suffering. Reality!

"All things are possible with our God!"

I am here to write you my heart desire—to see major change, to see Revival in Lansing. Sure I can dream of far away lands and distant dreams, but my heart goes out to the broken people of Lansing!

You are all so beautiful, lovely, and have amazing potential in JESUS!

Wake up Christians, no more lip service!

Live it out!

Roar, Daniel in the Lions' Den wants you to know that Jesus is real!

Experience Him with all your breath.

I don't know how much time we have. Serve Jesus today.

Seek Him while He may be found. Call on Him while He is near!

Meditate on things of God today!

I love you with all my heart. Hear me out. Jesus is the way!

Chapter 8 – FREE!

Many times the best things are free, but they do cost somebody something.

Somebody invested in you. Somebody laid down their lives, time, and money so that you could enjoy being "free!"

The Super Hero must understand this.

www.ingramcontent.com/pod-product-compliance
Lightning Source LLC
Chambersburg PA
CBHW070104290526
45789CB00005B/1917